JAPANESE EDUCATION

Its Past and Present

by KAIGO Tokiomi

KOKUSAI BUNKA SHINKOKAI

(Japan Cultural Society)

Tokyo, 1968

First edition, 1965
Second edition, 1968

Published by KOKUSAI BUNKA SHINKOKAI, *55, 1-chome, Shiba Shirokane-daimachi,
Minato-ku, Tokyo, Japan. Distributed by* JAPAN PUBLICATIONS TRADING COM-
PANY, *Central P.O. Box 722, Tokyo; 1255 Howard Street, San Francisco, Cali-
fornia 94103; 175 Fifth Avenue, New York, New York 10010. Copyright ©
1965 by Kokusai Bunka Shinkokai; all rights reserved. Printed in Japan.*

LCC Card No. 68-27305

It has long been regretted that students and scholars who engage in Japanese studies have to face many difficulties, not only in having to master a difficult language, but also in the matter of the lack of effective assistance by the learned institutions and people of this country. Recognizing this fact, the Kokusai Bunka Shinkokai (Japan Cultural Society), since shortly after its establishment in 1934, has been applying its energies to several programs for providing such facilities for foreign students and friends of Japan.

Initially the Society made a collection of Western-language books and magazines relating to Japan, which are available for reference at the K.B.S. Library, and published a full catalogue of the items collected during the years 1935–62, *A Classified List of Books in Western Languages Relating to Japan,* which is obtainable from the University of Tokyo Press.

Concurrently, since 1959 the Society has been compiling a series of bibliographies, under the series title *A Bibliography of Standard Reference Books for Japanese Studies with Descriptive Notes,* listing and describing the more important books written on Japan in Japanese. This is proving another valuable contribution to Japanese studies. Volumes already published cover the following fields: Generalia, Geography and Travel, History and Biography, Religion, History of Thought, Education, Language, Literature, Arts and Crafts, Theatre-Dance-Music, Manners and Customs and Folklore. In preparation are volumes covering: Politics, Law, and Economy.

Since 1961 the Society has also been publishing a series of books on Japanese life and culture, including the present publication, which give basic guidance in introductor fields of Japanese studies. Out of more than fifteen such published studies, the Society has now selected a number, as listed on the first page of this volume, which have been revised and reissued. More volumes, both revised and original editions, will appear successively. It is the sincere hope of the Society that this series, as well as its other activities, may prove of value to all who are interested in the study of Japan.

Mr. KAIGO Tokiomi, former professor of education at the University of Tokyo, is recognized as one of Japan's leading scholars in the field of pedagogy and has written several books and articles on the historical development of Japanese education.

Our acknowledgements are due to Dr. Alfred Bloom, of the University of Oregon, for his efficient and faithful translation of the text, and to Dr. Daniel R. Mansergh, Mr. Dixon Morris, and Mr. Norman F. Hallett for editorial assistance.

Two editorial notes: 1) The Hepburn system, with minor modifications, has been followed in romanizing Japanese words. 2) In the matter of Japanese personal names, the text of this book departs somewhat from our standard practice of using only the Japanese style (family name first) and uses the Western style for post-1868 persons.

September, 1968   KOKUSAI BUNKA SHINKOKAI

Contents

The educational setup was not yet organized. Education
was carried out in practical, daily experiences.

The nobles studied poetry and music following the pattern
of study of T'ang China. Schools as institutions of education were first established in this period. In the capital a
college termed *daigaku,* and in the provinces provincial
schools called *kokugaku,* were set up.

The warriors themselves trained their children in the military arts of archery, horsemanship and combat. In order to
provide literary studies they sent their children to Buddhist
temples. Towards the end of the Muromachi period (1333–
1573), the common people also began to send their children
to the temples to learn reading and writing.

The shogunate and local lords provided schools for their
warriors to study the literary and military arts, while the
common people attended the temple schools called *terakoya*
in order to learn reading, writing and the use of the abacus
(mathematics). These were very popular at the end of the

Tokugawa regime. Some institutions for social education were also founded.

necessary for the state. Many universities were created thereafter. In addition, advanced schools for general education and special colleges were also established.

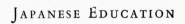

JAPANESE EDUCATION

CHAPTER I

Education in the Ancient Period

In early times, the Japanese, like other peoples, led a primitive existence. In such an age, individuals were mainly concerned with the problems of their everyday life. Their most basic problem was to secure food, and they worked strenuously in order to secure provisions, whether by means of cultivation, gathering seaweed and sea food, or by hunting animals. To learn where and how to secure their food required considerable knowledge and skills which they passed on to their children. Though their needs were very simple, they had to instruct their children in the methods of making clothes and in choosing a dwelling. The children imitated the skills of their parents and elder brothers or sisters as they lived together and sought to secure food and shelter for their daily lives. This was a mode of education carried out within and through their way of life. Institutions with the aim of educating did not exist in that early age in Japan.

In this period when stone implements were employed, skill in fashioning tools for their way of life was promoted. Knowledge and skills were required to find the necessary materials as well as to split, sharpen and use them. As the primitive way of life was gradually elevated through the use of stone tools, it was necessary to transmit these skills to future generations. Since there were no organized educational institutions to ensure the transmission of these skills, the children imitated the same form generation after generation.

With the gradual advance of his way of life and through the use of earthenware implements, the mode of life of primitive man was changed.

He rose above the stage of simple acquisition of clothing, food and shelter. For example, in the making of earthenware vessels, it was necessary to find good clay and a definite place to build a furnace to fire the pottery. Individuals specialized in making pots and earthenware implements. Since these skills also had to be passed down the generations, methods of teaching were established, and families who were noted for special skills in making such implements developed. In these particular families of experts, methods for teaching skills were gradually developed. However, this training was not carried out in an organized fashion. Since individuals of the next generation were permitted to participate in making utensils, the skills were naturally transmitted.

Fishing and crop harvesting reached a high level of proficiency during these early times. It was particularly necessary to transmit the methods of rice production such as tilling, sowing and harvesting to later generations. In order to provide education in the agricultural way of life, adults took the children with them into the fields.

Persons who had special skills gradually came to be formed into *be* (the guilds or corporations of workers, craftsmen, artists, etc., attached to the hereditary families or clans) in ancient Japan. There were numerous groups such as the *Hajibe* (earthenware-makers), *Suebe* (chinaware-makers), *Kagamitsukuribe* (mirror-makers), *Ishizukuribe* (masons), *Tamatsukuribe* (jewelry-makers), *Kinunuibe* (dressmakers), *Takumibe* (carpenters), *Nuribe* (lacquerer) and so on. These groups were organized into strong *bumin* (vocational clans) after about the fourth century A.D. The *bumin* who possessed various special skills lived as members of the court or as influential families. They highly prized and monopolized these special abilities which enabled them to establish their position. The documents of the Takahashi family (*Takahashi Uji Bumi*, 789 A.D.), which had charge of all that concerned the food of the court and competed with the Azumi clan in offering meals to the emperor, recorded, "In our country of Yamato, people are proud of their hereditary vocations." It is clear that a group would lose its reason for existence without a special skill since a clan's character was determined through the transmission of that skill from generation to generation. Consequently, the members of the clan highly prized the technique which constituted the vocational function of their family. It was regarded as the supporting pillar in the education of their children.

Technical skill had a very important meaning in ancient life since it made possible the production of tools for securing food, clothing and shelter, and resulted in the improvement of man's way of life. Furthermore, many special skills were transmitted by the *be* and through them the life of the *be* was elevated.

If we designate such skills as "arts" (*waza*), then we must recognize that the "arts" formed an important aspect in human education in this early period. Though the skills were simple in character, it took a great deal of time and effort to transmit them to the younger generation.

Each member of the clan had an "art" by which he established his position in the clan. Eventually these people formed a group and lived together in a specific place. The leader who could command and control the men of the clan was called the clan head or *uji no kami* or *tomo no o* when he represented the clan. The patriarch of such a clan clearly had to possess superior skill in the art possessed by his clan. In addition, he had to manifest powers of leadership which caused the members of the clan to obey him. Such power had to be regarded as supernatural and be sufficient to arouse reverence and awe in the minds of clan members. Through such mystical methods as divination by burning deer bones, the patriarch made his decisions. His gift of prophecy was adequate evidence to indicate to the clan members that he possessed supernatural powers.

Faith in the gods which existed from ancient times in Japan was developed from the veneration given, according to the situation, to superior persons and ancestral gods of the clan. Through such belief the men of the tribe could be controlled. The presence of religious beliefs is confirmed by the discovery of many ritual vessels. In view of the background of the ancestral cult it was natural that the patriarch of the clan should perform rituals and prayers. The leaders of the clans who settled western Japan were priests, and it is recorded that they were equipped with spiritual powers and the privilege of contacting the gods. The concept of the soul, the idea of pacifying the spirits, and the strengthening of the group consciousness of the members of the clan through reverence of ancestral gods were cultivated by those who contacted such gods. In earliest times liturgical invocations (*norito*) and the ideas and methods of purification from pollution were developed. The clan head became the leader of the clan through such religious practices.

Those who had the privilege of worshipping the gods in this manner had to transmit this knowledge to succeeding generations. Those who were selected to inherit the position of clan head were given a priestly education in religious methods and the words to worship the gods. This was the highest form of education in ancient society. But again there were no special educational institutions to accomplish this. Such education was taken up in the religious rituals themselves, and it was an education gained through the activity of the liturgy (*matsuri*) as members of the clan sat in a row during the service. Those who sat received the spiritual side of their education through observing the ritual.

Education for the members of the ancient clans was based on the "arts" (*waza*) and the "liturgy" (*matsuri*). However, there were no special educational institutions set up for that purpose. Rather, education was largely based on imitation by the children of the activities that took place in everyday life.

CHAPTER II

Education of the Nobility

The aristocrats described those superior persons who were well educated by such terms as "excellent in *zae* (intellectuality) and *katachi* (appearance)". Here *zae* referred to scholarship and artistic achievement, while *katachi* expressed one's refinement which was revealed in one's countenance, as well as one's bearing and behaviour.

When we look into the *Family Biography (Kaden)* which relates the life of Fujiwara no Kamatari (A.D. 614–669), we are told that Minister Kamatari, who was a representative aristocrat, was "benevolent in nature, very intelligent and highly scholarly. He loved learning from his childhood and read many books in numerous fields. He had a very elegant and grand air. Especially he excelled in his deportment". This is a description of Kamatari's superior personality as a human being, and most felicitous words were chosen to depict his great character.

Also, in the *Kimpishô*[1] of Emperor Juntoku (1210–1221), there are notations concerning the various arts. These are divided generally into scholarship and music. The text makes clear the most desirable ways for accomplishing those arts. Scholarship was regarded as very important in the education of a noble person. One could not comprehend classical learning without study. It was demanded that one should by all means memorize the *Gunsho Chiyô*[2] even though he might not progress to the point of mastering the *Keishi*.[3]

---

1 Excerpts on Court Affairs, 1218–1221.
2 *Ch'un-shu Chih-yao*, excerpts on T'ang politics, A.D. 633.
3 Ancient Chinese classics.

In the study of music, it was required that one be well versed in at least one repertoire. Various types of instruments were the flute, the *wagon* or *yamato-goto* (Japanese harp with six strings), the *sô* (harp with thirteen strings), the *biwa* (lute), the *shô* (mouth pipe organ) and the *hichiriki* (small reed pipe). *Waka* (Japanese poetry), Chinese poetry and calligraphy were similarly indicated as necessary requirements in the arts.

These notations reveal the various artistic skills which the aristocrats were to possess. Through these we can observe what kind of learning comprised the education of a noble of that period.

At that time noble ladies were also required to have skills in calligraphy, the composition of Japanese poems and other arts. It is stated in the *Makura-no-Sôshi* (Pillow Book of Sei Shônagon):

First learn calligraphy and then try to be superior to others in playing the harp. Finally you should include in your learning the memorization of the twenty volumes of the *Kokinshû*.[1]

This passage depicts the necessary elements in the education of girls who would enter the life of the court.

In conformity with this object of acquiring the refinements involved in intellect and appearance, the aristocrats of the period tried to train their children in scholarly achievements. When the children of aristocrats became five years of age, a ritual ceremony was held to mark the beginning of their education. This event was considered the first step in the pursuit of scholarship. On that occasion scholars were invited to the homes of the nobles as tutors. The ceremony consisted of reading and interpreting stanzas of the *Hsiao Ching*.[2] In order to provide further education, advanced schools were established.

An important aspect of the education of the nobility lies in their schools which were set up and administered as a national system. The establishment of the national school system is attested to in the provision of the education law of the famous Taihô Code (A.D. 701) in accordance with which a college was founded in the capital and in each of the provincial

---

1 Anthology of Japanese Poems, ancient and modern, A.D. 905.
2 Book of Filial Piety, a Confucian classic. See the chart in p. 9

areas. From these institutions schools for educating the aristocrats developed.

However, it is generally accepted that the first establishment of schools in Japan was actually much earlier than the promulgation of this law. It is said that the Hôryû Gakumonji[1] set up by Prince Shôtoku was the first. However, this school was merely for study in the Temple. It cannot, therefore, be considered as an independent school in the ordinary sense of the word. Although it can be inferred that scholars who came to Hôryûji from the Chinese continent gave scholarly lectures, it had not yet become recognized as a regular school.

The first school in Japan was the institution which is thought to have been established at Ômi in the time of Emperor Tenchi (A.D. 662–671). A note concerning this school in the preface of the Kaifûsô[2] relates that schools were established at that time and there was considerable progress in education. Also from the name of the office called Fumuya Zukasa no Kami (Director of School Education) it is evident that schools were set up and administered by the Imperial Court. Soon thereafter in the fourth year of Emperor Temmu (A.D. 676), we are told that a college with professors and students who pursued academic learning already existed. Since we can affirm the existence of a so-called daigaku (大學) or college in this period, we may also safely infer that a school corresponding to the daigakuryô (大學寮) or college-house had already been established previously in the capital from the time of Emperor Tenchi (A.D. 662–671). It was this institution which was later stipulated by the school law in the Taihô Code (A.D. 701), and for a long time it played a central role in the education of the aristocratic class.

Turning to the function of the daigakuryô as an educational institution for the nobility, we may observe that according to the personnel regulation of teachers and administrators provided in the Taihô Code, there were various administrative officials, each having a title such as daigaku

---

1 At that time, Hôryûji temple did not belong to any particular sect of Buddhism and was a monastic school. Therefore, it was called Hôryû Gakumon(learning)-ji.

2 The oldest anthology of Japanese verse composed in Chinese style, compiled in A.D. 751.

no kami (rector), *suke* (vice rector), *tai-jô* (upper head), *shô-jô* (lower head), *tai-sakan* (upper sub-official) and *shô-sakan* (lower sub-official). In addition, it was stipulated that there should be appointed one professor, two assistants, four hundred students of classical learning; two professors of music; two professors of literature and calligraphy; two professors and thirty students of mathematics. The professors and their assistants engaged in the actual teaching.

Later, such positions as *myôhô hakase* (doctor of laws), *kiden hakase* (doctor of history), and *bunjô hakase* (doctor of literature) were formulated and the scope of instruction in the *daigakuryô* broadened.

The fourfold division of the arts consisted in the interpretation of Confucian scriptures *(myôkyô)*, interpretation of law *(myôhô)*, composition *(monjô)* and mathematics *(san)*. The study of *monjô* was regarded as most important.

As a rule, the students who enrolled in the *daigakuryô* were children from the fifth rank and above as well as those of the *Fubitobe* (learned men) of Yamato-Kawachi. If the children of those persons above the eighth rank expressed a desire, they could also be enrolled according to regulation.

Students were required to master one of the following classical texts: *Shûeki* (周易), *Shôsho* (尚書), *Shûrai* (周禮), *Girai* (儀禮), *Raiki* (禮記), *Môshi* (毛詩) and *Shunjû Sashiden* (春秋左氏伝). At the same time every student learned *Kôkyô* (孝経) and *Rongo* (論語). The scholia of Cheng Hüan (鄭玄) and Wang Pi (王弼) were customarily used as commentaries. These ancient classics were classified into *Daikyô* (Great Classics) including *Raiki* and *Shunjû Sashiden*, the *Chûkyô* (Middle Classics) which is comprised of the *Môshi*, *Shûrai* and *Girai*, and the *Shôkyô* (Small Classics) which includes the *Shûeki* and *Shôsho*. While the curriculum was organized according to these divisions, the level of scholarship was determined by what texts the student had mastered. At a later time the required length of time for the study of each classic was fixed, and the standard for promotion established.

After becoming able to read the classics, the students would discuss their meaning. Every ten days there was a one day vacation. The day before there would be an examination. Furthermore, at the end of the year there was a test over all they had been taught. For those who tried to become public officials a promotion system in imitation of the T'ang was applied after they became well-versed in more than two Chinese classics. The details of the promotion system were given in the laws of selection and aptitude tests. There were six types of tests, namely, *shûsai* (planning and strategy), *myôkyô (Chinese classics)*, *shinshi* (politics), *myôhô* (law), *sho* (calligraphy) and *san* (mathematics). Individuals were divided into ranks according to their merits in each of these areas. It became a principle that one received his rank according to his depth of scholarship.

At that time there was also *on-i* which is a rank based on the merit of

CHINESE CLASSICS			
		Appelations in Chinese & Japanese	Curriculum
A. Five Classics	(五經)		
(1) *Classic of Documents*	(書經)	Shü ching, Shokyô	Small Classics (小經) Shôkyô
or	(尚書)	Shang shü, Shôsho	
(2) *Classic of Changes*	(易經)	I ching, Ekikyô	
or	(周易)	Choü i, Shûeki	Great Classics (大經) Daikyô
(3) *Spring and Autumn Annals*	(春秋)	Ch'ün ch'iü, Shunjû	
(4) *Record of Rituals*	(禮記)	Li chi, Raiki	
(a) *Great Learning*	(大學)	Ta hsüeh, Daigaku	
(b) *Doctrine of the Mean*	(中庸)	Chüng yung Chûyô	
(5) *Classic of Songs*	(詩經)	Shin ching, Shikyô	
or	(毛詩)	Mao shih, Môshi	
B. Thirteen Classics	(十三経)		Middle Classics (中經) Chûkyô
Beside the seven books (dividing *Spring and Autumn Annals* into three books) of the Five Classics, the following six books are included:			
(8) *Ceremonies and Rituals*	(儀禮)	I li, Girai	
(9) *Rituals of Chou*	(周禮)	Chou li, Shûrai	
(10) *Analects*	(論語)	Lun yü, Rongo	
(11) *Mencius*	(孟子)	Meng-tze, Môshi	
(12) *Classic of Filial Piety*	(孝經)	Hsiao ching, Kôkyô	
(12) *Etymological Dictionary*	(爾雅)	Erh ya, Jiga	
C. Four Books	(四書)		
(1) *Great Learning* (A-4-a)	(大學)	Ta hsüeh, Daigaku	
(2) *Doctrine of the Mean* (A-4-b)	(中庸)	Chüng yung, Chûyô	
(3) *Analects* (B-10)	(論語)	Lun yü, Rongo	
(4) *Mencius* (B-11)	(孟子)	Meng-tze, Môshi	

one's ancestors. Sons of the nobility received investiture according to the rank of his family. Since this rank was comparatively higher that the rank received according to the promotion system of the *daigakuryô*, we can conclude that an aristocrat did not enter the *daigakuryô* only for the sake of promotion.

The provincial schools *(kokugaku)* were institutions of learning provided for those living in the respective provinces. There were differences between the Dazaifu[1] and each province concerning the way in which the provincial schools were set up. Since the school of Dazaifu[1] was set up for the sake of the entire Kyushu area, the organization was larger and included one professor, one teacher of *on'yô* (astrology and calendar), two medical doctors, and one doctor of mathematics. In the provincial schools there was a provincial professor and a doctor of medicine.

Besides the children of the county head *(gunji)* who were allowed to enter the school, the most intelligent children between thirteen and sixteen years of age were also permitted to attend. The students consisted of fifty from the greatest provinces, forty from the greater provinces, thirty from the middle-sized provinces and twenty from the small provinces. It was also determined that one fifth of the students must take the medical course.

A summary of the regulations governing the curriculum of the college and the provincial schools indicates that divination and medicine were offered in the provincial schools, while these studies were carried out in the capital in several schools apart from the *daigakuryô*. Medicine was studied in the bureau of pharmacy *(tenyakuryô)*, divination *(in'yô)*, calendar *(koyomi)* and astrology *(temmon)* in the bureau of divination *(in'yôryô)*, and music education in the bureau of music *(gagakuryô)*. Consequently, the Taihô Code made the classics central in the educational curriculum of the *daigakuryô* in the metropolitan area. However, the provisions of the code generally extended to the various other schools in the capital.

---

1 An early government office for military and diplomatic service, established by the Yamato court in the present town of the same name in Kyushu.

The schools of the capital were very well organized for the children of the nobility. However, this system of schools based on the T'ang system could not be permanently enforced just as it was. The famous twelve article memorial to the government by Miyoshi Kiyoyuki (A.D. 914) described the run-down condition of the *daigakuryô*. Since this was a situation some two hundred years after the Taihô period, we cannot generalize on the actual conditions of the institution for the whole period. However, the *daigakuryô* did not flourish greatly, and appears to have been declining even when Fujiwara no Muchimaro became Vice Rector in the Taihô period (701–703). Thus, it was not greatly prospering even at the time that the law was given. Nevertheless, it is particularly noteworthy that until it was destroyed by fire in the Jishô period (A.D. 1171) it continuously functioned as the school of the capital.

The children of the nobility lived in the *daigakuryô*, and lodgings where they could pursue their studies were provided. These were called *zôshi*. Looked at from the standpoint of today they doubled as dormitories and places of study. There were two kinds of *zôshi*: the *jikisô* established within the college and the *bessô* outside the *daigakuryô*. The Ôe and Sugawara families both administered the *jikisô*. The *bessô* were provided by each influential family, and the children of those families lived and studied together.

The earliest among the *bessô* was the Kôbun'in of Wake no Hiroyo. This was the residence for the students of the Wake family, and it was located south of the *daigakuryô*. To pursue their education the children of the Wake clan commuted to the *daigaku* where they received instruction from the professors. It is also recorded that several thousands of foreign and domestic books were stored there. Educational expenses were supplied for a long time by the income from forty hectars of their rice fields.

The Kangaku'in was the largest and most famous among the *bessô*, and it continued the longest. This was the *zôshi* for the students of the Fujiwara clan. Fujiwara no Fuyutsugu established it in A.D. 821. It was called Daigakuryô Nansô (Southern annex of the Daigakuryô). A *bettô* and *gakutô* were appointed to head this fairly large institution. Several men of great intelligence of the Fujiwara clan were educated in this school. Just as it was said in a proverb that the sparrows near the Kan-gaku'in naturally recited the Chinese classics, so many Fujiwara children studied and recited them here. In addition, there were other *zôshi* such as the Shôgakuin of the Ariwara clan and the Gakkan'in of the Tachibana family.

These academies were established in affiliation with the *daigakuryô* which was a national institution. Besides these, there were other privately established schools. A representative one was the Shugeishuchiin established by the priest Kûkai. The general outline of its teaching and organization is extant in its rules and the rules' preface of A.D. 828 which were its basis. Accordingly, the *daigakuryô* alone was set up in the capital and there were no other schools at that time for those who were poor but aspired to an education. It was Kûkai's idea that the culture of a country could not be made to flourish in such a situation. Therefore, he copied the method of the village school (*lii shu*) of the T'ang and constructed places of study through which he tried to give the opportunity of education to the greatest number of people. It is related in the *Tôhôki* that after thirty years his school was sold and closed. But it is generally held that apart from the *daigakuryô*, private schools in Japan were first founded by Kûkai and specialists in Buddhism and Confucianism taught there.

Further, a study of Kûkai's rules and preface indicates that the Nikyôin of Kibi no Makibi and the Unteiin of Isonokami no Yakatsugu were actually established before Kûkai's school, but that neither of them continued for long. Perhaps these should be considered as schools also. Several examples indicate that students attended as disciples studying under the guidance of great scholars. In cases where scholarship for the nation was urgently needed, students received a wage in food and clothing in order to make it possible for them to study. For instance, it is recorded in the *Montoku Jitsuroku* (Record of the Montoku Period, A.D. 876) that Yoshida Tsureyoshi and others were training students in various fields such as divination, medicine, calendar, law. Thus, it is clear that places of scholarship and education of public signifcance were established outside the *daigakuryô*.

When we survey those educational institutions of the capital which centered in the *daigakuryô*, it appears that the education of the nobility took an extremely classical form based on the Chinese classics. However, the nobles did not intend to base the education of their children on such scholarship alone. As children of the nobility, they also had to have a broader cultural education for life in the court. We can observe this in such studies as *yûsoku kojitsu* (court practice), *monjôgaku* (rhetoric) *shigaku* (Chinese poetry), *kagaku* (Japanese poetry) and *shodô* (calligraphy).

Yûsoku kojitsu is learning related to court ceremonies and worship customs (liturgies). It had been organized based on the daily practices of each aristocratic family and the regular and annual rituals in the court. The most difficult among them concerned the *jimoku* (ceremonies of installation). We can infer their importance by the fact that many books relating to court practices remain until today.

How significant the scholarship relating to literature and the cultural qualities indicated by it were, can easily be understood from the way of life of the nobility. Rhetoric and composition was especially highly regarded in the *daigakuryô*. The professor of rhetoric received a high rank which indicates that rhetoric and composition were more highly respected than the study of Chinese classical literature. The *monjô hakase* or professor of rhetoric was the central position in the school.

The terms *shi* and *monjô* refer to Chinese poems and prose respectively, and they were studied either in the homes of scholars in those areas or in public institutions. Many students gathered and studied under men who were famous for their ability at writing. Also many were trained with scholars who had studied on the continent. We can learn how hard the nobles worked to learn to write from such works as the *Honchômonzui* (Selected Writings of Japanese Authors, ed. by Fujiwara no Akihira) in which representative pieces were gathered and edited in 9th–11th century.

Together with writing prose, poetry making formed one important aspect of the education of aristocarts. Extant poems which may be read today testify to their great efforts. The most outstanding collections remaining to the present are the *Ryôunshû*,[1] *Bunka Shûreishû*[2] and the *Keikokushû*.[3] We may estimate the important role of poetry and literature in the general education of the time from the popularity of Po Lê-tien's writings and the widely read *Anthology of Japanese and Chinese Poetry*. Po Lê-tien was especially well known. The importance of poetry is also seen in the fact that the test for candidates to be scribes *(monjô-sei)* included a knowledge of poetry. Many princes and aristocrats attended poetry meetings in the Imperial court and influential families in the court pitted themselves against each other in making poems.

The composition of Japanese poems *waka* was also highly regarded in the education of the aristocrat and even considered as the symbol of his way of life. We are unable to grasp exactly the level of the culture of the noble without understanding that the life of a noble depended on Japanese poetry. *Waka* was used not only as an instrument to describe in an elegant manner natural and human affairs, but it was also a means of communicating one's intention and thought to his partner in all kinds of situations both in the official life of the court and the private life of the family. Thus, the *waka* had a tremendous importance in all aspects of aristocratic life.

It should be especially noted that *uta-awase* (group contests for composing poetry) were frequently held in each house of the nobility and formed one aspect of their lives. It became an indispensable element of the education of a noble to improve his ability in making impromptu poems of high quality at such ceremonious occasions as were sometimes held in official buildings or at the Imperial court. Special attention, therefore, was paid to learning Japanese poetry from childhood. The *waka* poems of "Naniwazu" and Asakayama" were the first to be learned by the young, and they were the models for composition.

---

1 An anthology of the first ninety Chinese-style poems of the early Heian period (782-814 A.D.) selected by Sugawara-no Kiyokimi. The 23 poets were emperors and government officials.

2 An anthology of Chinese-style poems in three volumes compiled in 818 A.D. by Fujiwara-no Fuyutsugu by Imperial order. The 143 poems composed by 26 poets are listed.

3 A collection of Chinese-style poems and prose of the early Heian period selected by Yoshimine-no Yasuyo and others in 827 by Imperial order, compiled in 20 volumes.

In connection with the learning of Japanese poems, Fujiwara no Moto-toshi stated in his *Etsumokushô:*

The most important thing in this study is to recite and master ancient poems... In short, begin with the *Manyôshû* (Anthology of Myriad Leaves) and master the *Sandaishû* (Anthology of the Three Eras, i.e. *Kokin-wakashû, Gosenshû, Shûi-wakashû*) to penetrate the meaning and methods of ancient poetic expression.

Many collections of Japanese poetry were used as text books. The *Manyôshû* and the *Kokinshû* (Anthology of Poems, Ancient and Modern) were held most fundamental. Learning by memorizing them completely was the basic method in all studies. At the same time, poetical stories as the *Ise Monogatari* and the *Yamato Monogatari* were also used as texts to help the nobles understand the meaning of the poems in their lives. There are many books written in this period in which the basic principles of Japanese poetry were held as esoteric teachings of particular families. They indicate the ways of mastering poetry in this period.

Observing how industriously the nobles laboured to demonstrate their superior ability in mastering Japanese poetic composition, we are able to understand the importance of such study for human education.

Shodô (penmanship or calligraphy) could not be separated from the practice of poetry, and *waka* formed an important element in the educa-tion of the nobles. Lessons in penmanship began with the practising simplified letters of *kana,* employing the Japanese alphabet songs such as "Iroha" and the "Ametsuchi". After mastering the lessons, they practised cursive penmanship by copying such *waka* poems as "Naniwazu" or "Asakayama". Following that they took many advanced courses.

In the case of boys it was required to learn to write *kanji* (Chinese characters). They began to learn to write Chinese characters: first learn-ing the *gyôsho* or semi-cursive style, then progressing to *sôsho* or cursive and *kaisho* or standard styles. Poems were frequently used as material. Such works as the *Anthology of Japanese and Chinese Poems* provided important materials for the practice of calligraphy.

Superior skill in writing was required in the way of life of the nobility. Such texts of Imperial Rescripts and political orders as *semmyô, senji,*

shohyô, jijô and môshibumi, and the religious writings of invocations
(gammon) and copied sutras required superior skill in writing and indicated the personality of the nobles. There was a definite method and
style in the laws in writing those documents which contained standards
for such things as the form of the character and usage. Therefore, students
were obliged to make extraordinary efforts in learning how to write
them correctly and beautifully.

The three aspects of the position, motion and touch of the brush were
especially valued in the method of writing, and the students applied
themselves diligently to their practice. As they penetrated deeper into the
secrets of calligraphy, they cultivated one stage after the other, finally
reaching a stage which is inexpressible by words. Thus, together with the
fact that writing was a necessity in the way of life of the noble, it also was
valued highly as a way of the cultivation of his personality. Later, such
works as the *Hidensho* (esoteric teaching of calligraphy) came to be
produced.

Together with the learning and composition of poems, music was one
of the necessary requirements of the nobles. In speaking of their education one hears such expressions as "he is superior in the three aspects of
shi-ka-kangen (poem, song and music)". The nobles who were endowed
with these three talents were respected and called *sansen-no-zae* (talent of
three ships).[1] Besides scholarship and poetry, *kangen* or music (literally:
wind and string instruments) was particularly esteemed in the education
of the aristocrat. This musical sphere of education was called *kangen.*
The system of education in music was established very early. In the Taihô
Cord (701 A.D.) there was a provision relative to the *Gagakuryô* (department of court music). Here various teachers of musical instruments were
designated. Students who wanted to study particular musical instruments
were attached to those teachers. It was a system relative to the education
of musicians or specialists in music. Hence, it must be considered separately from the general musical training of the children of the aristocrats.

---

1 In 1083 Emperor Shirakawa made a journey to Oseki River, where three ships were
prepared for poetry, singing and playing musical instruments respectively. It is the origin
of the tradition of the "talent of three ships".

As is indicated in the statement: "There is nothing superior to music to cultivate one's mind all the time and to bequeath one's name (fame) to the following generation", music was greatly valued among the accomplishments of the noble. Besides making merry, individuals at a banquet played their favourite instruments, thereby boasting the height of their education in their own skills.

The instruments most used at the time and most familiar to the children of the nobles were the *koto* (harp), *fue* (flute) and *biwa* (lute). Among the types of "koto", *wagon* (Japanese harp with six strings), *sô* (harp with thirteen strings) and *kin* (harp with seven strings) can be distinguished. They used *fue* (traverse flute), *shakuhachi* (flute à bec) and *hichiriki* (small reed pipe) as wind instruments. Besides these they also learned the *biwa* (lute) and *taiko* (drum). In order to learn these, they had excellent instruments and chose famous artists as teachers. However, some musical forms could be mastered only after life-long training.

In addition to those studies, they learned such things as drawing, incense mixing, cooking, football, falconry, archery and horsemanship as artistic achievements of the nobles. In this way they cultivated their several abilities. All of these were called learning or achievement in arts. It is very clear that the concept of learning at that time covered an extremely wide area.

Education in *katachi* or bearing comprehended everything from dress and its ornaments and the manner of wearing them to one's whole appearance and deportment. It was required that individuals be superior even in their appearance or bearing. Education in these aspects was achieved naturally in their homes and by participating in various functions in the court and in the homes of influential families.

The aristocrats formulated such education but it was not established only as a mode of education peculiar to the nobility. At that time the common people looked upon the noble as his superior, and they demanded an education following a pattern similar to that of the nobility. Consequently, in order to judge whether or not a person had a high education, one employed these patterns of the nobles as criteria. He endeavoured to live accordingly in the belief that it was a necessity. As is mentioned above, the nobles said those who excelled in poems, songs, and music were endowed with the talent of "three ships". They competed against each other in "floating three ships", choosing one of them according to their likes and pitting their ability against each other. Many persons watched these contests, and probably aspired to education in one of those studies. Consequently, even among the common people the value of a person was recognized by his possessing superior ability in the arts of poems, songs and musical instruments. Among the narratives of life in that period, there are some stories in which common people who excelled to some degree in those arts attained great fame by their skill. For example, there is a story about a child of a woodsman who recited splendid poetry *(waka)*. There is also a story of a farmer who was superior in playing the flute and became famous on that account; again a story of a soldier who came to the capital from a province and on hearing the theme of a poetry contest before the gate of an influential family, won the prize by immediately improvising an excellent *waka*. These incidents indicate that the people of that time achieved an education based entirely on the educational methods of the nobility. Therefore, the education, which the nobility who had the power to govern devised from within their own way of life, determined the method which became the basis for the education of men generally in that age. The education of the nobility was unique in having the life of the court as its foundation, but the education required of these aristocrats also became the basis for the way of thinking concerning education for all persons of that age.

CHAPTER III

Education of Warriors

The medieval warrior families traditionally described superior individuals as those who had a brave and courageous spirit, and excelled in archery and horsemanship. Minamoto no Yoritomo (1147–1199) demanded three qualities in his bodyguards which the *Azuma Kagami*[1] terms being "proficient in the three virtues". These three virtues were: to be a man of a courageous family, to be excellent in archery and horsemanship, and to be restrained in behaviour.

Although these qualities were requirements of Yoritomo's bodyguards, they were an expression of what was desired in a warrior generally. The warriors called themselves the "family of archery and horsemanship," and they regarded expertness in these activities as the most appropriate attributes of a warrior. They defined their difference from the nobility as the way of battling with archery and horsemanship as is stated in the *Yoshisadaki* (義貞記):[2]

> From ancient times until the present day, military arms and the pen have been considered as two virtues like heaven and earth. Lacking one of them, one cannot control the affairs of a state. Therefore, the nobles primarily engage in literature and learn such arts as poetry-making and music. But for statesmen arms are of the utmost importance. These consist of archery, horsemanship and strategy.

---

1 A book of history of the Kamakura shogunate arranged in chronological order, covering the years 1180-1266. The author is unknown.
2 Chronicle of Nitta Yoshisada (1301-1338), contained in *Gunsho Ruijû.*

Later in the *Buke Shohatto*[1] we read in article 1:

They should practise solely pen and arms, archery and horsemanship. There is added the clause:

Archery and horsemanship are the most essential skills of warriors. These statements reveal clearly how the warriors regarded their qualities, and it is a very important point in considering the unique mode of the education of the warrior.

Such military arts as archery and horsemanship were central in the achievements of the warriors, but they did not reject culture entirely or fail to take notice of it. Education in letters was required along with military arts, but cultivation of skill in warfare was primary. In the notation for the second year of Kenchô (1250) in the *Azuma Kagami,* it is recorded that Hôjô Tokiyori (1227–1263) advised the Shogun that there should be training in both cultural and military arts. Both teachers of Japanese and Chinese poetry and teachers of archery and horsemanship were to be sent to the place. This description reveals the essential points of the education of a shogun who had to excel as a warrior and also achieve refinement. This viewpoint became the standard for the education of the warrior class, and in writings of the time we frequently find such terms as "the two paths of culture and military arts". "Left-culture, Right-military arts", or "Proficient both in culture and military arts". In "the *21 family precepts of Hôjô Sôun* (1432–1519)" we read:

Culture and military arts, archery and horsemanship, are to be studied constantly. It is an ancient custom that, on one hand, one should study letters, and on the other hand, the military arts. They should be mastered at the same time.

Here is recognition that the correct education of a warrior included both cultural and military arts. However, the military arts were regarded as the basic element in the education of the warrior. Thus, the warriors particularly concentrated their efforts on educating their children in the military arts of archery and horsemanship.

---

1 The regulations for warriors promulgated in 1615 by the Tokugawa shogunate.

Warriors were taught these various arts from their childhood. According to passages in the *Gempei Seisuiki*[1] where a description is given of Okazaki Bunzo's nurturing of his lord's child, it is stated:

As he became five or six years old, I taught him to take a small bow and arrows of small bamboo and to shoot at targets, deer targets, rabbits and to ride on horseback after rabbits and deer.

Even in play children attained familiarity with archery and horsemanship as they used bows and arrows and rode horses made of bamboo and grass. Many pictures from this period graphically portray the way in which the warriors educated their children.

The bamboo-grass horses and the bow in hand symbolized the way of life of warrior children. And as they grew up, even their spare time was taken up with training in these skills. For this purpose the warriors provided archery ranges and riding places in their estates. Archery and horsemanship were combined when warrior families competed against each other in contests held in the *bugeijô* (place of military arts). There the warriors gathered and demonstrated the skills which they practised daily.

Whenever there were Shinto or Buddhist festivals, activities in the military arts were sponsored in order to demonstrate the various skills. In the art of shooting, effort was concentrated chiefly on two types of contest, called: "three objects shot on foot" and, "three objects shot on horseback". The three objects shot in the standing position were the "large target" *(ômato)*, the deer target *(kusajishi)* and the round target *(marumono)*. The three shots while on horseback were the *yabusame* (three target shooting), *kasagake* (bamboo hat target shooting) and *inuoimono* (dog shooting).

The "large target" was round and about 62 inches across. The archery course was 33 bow lengths. Two archers stood together and competed. The deer target was composed of a deer drawn on wood and covered with skin. Various white spots on the body formed the "bull's eyes" of the target. Warriors competed trying to hit these markings. The contest was patterned after the method of hunting deer. The *marumono* was

---

1 *The Vicissitudes of the Genji and Heike Families*, compiled in the latter half of the Kamakura period; the author unknown.

made of a round board covered with hide. The skin was stuffed so as to form a hemisphere, which was hard to pierce with ordinary bows.

The three objects shot while on horseback combined both methods of shooting and riding. These were all competitive events carried out in the riding arena. In the *yabusame* participants shot at three targets in rapid succession. The targets were made of three inch square boards and placed at intervals along the riding ground which extended 109 metres. The bamboo hat target or *kasagake* involved targets shot at a distance *(tôkasagake)* and those closer *(kokasagake)*. A path for shooting called the *yadô* (arrow way) was constructed with fences in the riding arena. At the end of the *yadô* there was a shelf on which the bamboo hats were hung. In the feat of the *inuoimono* (dog shooting), which employed dogs as targets, thirty six mounted archers divided into three groups of twelve inside the riding arena composed of a circular bamboo fence 71 bow lengths across. Fifty dogs were released for each group and through the competition one's skill in archery and horsemanship was revealed. The dogs were shot with special non-deadly arrows with large round arrowheads so that the dogs shot were not killed.

Through daily practice, members of the warrior families received an education in the military arts. Other aspects of military training were the use of the sword, halberd and lance. Especially, much effort was put into training in swordsmanship because it was used extensively. Horse races were increasingly employed on ceremonial occasions. Such things as *sumô* (wrestling) may also be regarded as an activity for training warriors. The forty eight techniques of *sumô* were devised about this time.

Education in the military arts mentioned above was not the only means to train warriors, but it was always required that a more practical system of training giving battle field experience be combined with these military arts. Ultimately the warrior had as his aim to act as a superior warrior on the battlefield and to brighten the honour of his family by making his name remembered in later generations.

Since opportunity of actual battle was not always available, other methods were employed to give training resembling actual battle conditions. Among these were *oitorigari* (bird hunting) and *makigari* (grand hunt) which were carried out in the open field. The warriors stayed for a definite period in an encampment away from Kamakura. There they competed by exhibiting the skills they had learned in methods of warfare. For a famous hunt at the foot of mount Fuji, many warriors, including the Shogun himself, came from Kamakura and set up camp. The men vied for merit in driving out birds and animals and shooting them down. The warriors who took deer and wild boar attained honour just as if they had killed an enemy general. To catch these birds and animals it was necessary to have the same bravery which was demanded on the battlefield. The story, in which Yoritomo reported to his wife Masako in Kamakura through an emissary from Mt. Fuji the success of their son in shooting a deer, shows how highly such feats were regarded and how much effort was put into them.

Since the object of such training in the military arts in the field was to prepare the warrior for the battlefield, we can understand the great attention given them. They provided the best opportunities to practise and perfect military techniques, and the earnestness of the warrior education can be discovered here. When a son of a warrior became thirteen or fourteen years old, he accompanied his father to the field. When he passed his tenth year a special celebration was held to mark his coming of age and he was made to assume the responsibilities of an adult warrior.

Performance on the battlefield itself was of utmost importance, and there were frequent incidents related in which the young warrior fought with great valour. For example, it is narrated in the *Mutsuwaki*[1] that the thirteen-year-old son of Abe no Sadatô by the name of Senze Dôshi went into battle. He was handsome and wore armour. Stepping out of the barrier he fought courageously in the way of his ancestors. He was finally captured, but when the shogun observed that he was only a young warrior, he was hesitant in beheading the boy. These accounts describe well the last moment of this young warrior. In the *Gempei Seisuiki* there

---

1 A story of war in 1051-1062, called the First Nine Years' War, waged by Minamoto-no Yoriyoshi (998-1075) against Abe-no Yoritoki and his sons, Sadatô and Munesada. The author unknown.

is also the story of Kumagai on the occasion of the attack on the routed
Heike clan. There was a conference in the *Samuraidokoro* (warriors'
quarters) of the Kamakura palace before they proceeded to the western
provinces in pursuit of the Heike. It was decided that only warriors above
seventeen years of age should go up to the capital. At that time Kojiro,
the son of Kumagai Naozane was just sixteen years old and he knew he
would not be permitted to go. Claiming that he was seventeen he went
along to the capital. His father's attitude on that occasion was recorded as
follows: "I thought that he might learn war..." This shows well the
idea of the warrior that to learn the art of war one must accompany the
army to the battlefield as soon as possible.

During battle the military arts which the children had learned were
supported by spiritual attitudes. These were all united together in the
discipline of the children. The spirit most honoured on the battlefield was
the determination to honour one's family name. In the *Shômonki*[1] it states
that the soldier puts his name first above all else. They were severely
admonished against staining names. It was firmly believed that the
warrior's honourable duty lay in fighting heartily and giving one's life
for his lord. The warrior regulations of the *Mutsuwaki* state:

> Now I abandon my life for the sake of my shogun. My life is as light
> as a hair of a crane. I prefer to die facing my enemy than to live by
> turning my back to him.

Such statements indicate the resolution of the warrior, and this spirit was
forged by placing their children in a way of life in which they fought
with a sense of gratitude and a willingness to offer their lives. The father
admonished his son; the elder brother discussed it with his younger
brother. They considered it most shameful to live by retreating and most
honourable to die advancing. They thought that to refrain from shameful acts was the only way to repay one's obligation to one's lord.

The warriors were first trained in this spirit in the practice of fighting
and exercises in the military arts, but it was actually comprehended

---

1 The first war literature written in 940 by an unknown author. A history of the mid-
Heian civil war caused by Taira-no Masakado (-940).

during battle when they risked their very lives. A truly serious education was required for this. The military arts actually became their own as they really engaged in fierce battle. The warriors naturally considered such opportunities for the education of their sons as most valuable, and they always sought for such occasions. Here one can see their practical attitude towards education.

In normal times the education of the children was cared for at home, and the warriors always set the example as they undertook the entire discipline of their kinsmen and vassals. It was of major importance that the warrior always took the initiative as the centre of the daily discipline. This initiative in peace time was in unity with the mode of education on the battlefield where the warrior led his retainers. In books of precepts made for warrior children, we can frequently observe that the parents undertook the education of their children in every phase of daily life. Warrior families formulated precepts and rules which all members had to follow and which expressed the fundamental attitude of the parents.

In addition, unique methods for educating the children in letters were developed by the warrior families. We may note that while the warriors pursued education in letters in their way of life, they did not establish special schools for that purpose as the nobility did. Since the warriors did not regard scholarship as the chief purpose of life, they did not demand it in the instructional methods of their schools.

Nevertheless, since education in letters was constantly required in connection with their life as warriors, they endeavoured to achieve ability in this area, too. Because the shogun regarded the best education in letters a necessity, we can survey the opportunities which existed in his family in order to see how such cultural training was done. Some passages in the *Azuma Kagami* refer to occasions of cultural training. Meetings for composing *waka* became increasingly popular. There were convivia of Japanese poetry in the house of Ôe no Hiromoto. On that occasion, copies of the *Sandaishû* (Anthology of Three Generations) were given as prizes. Also in the shogun's house, discussions which employed books relating to political matters were frequently held. There are notations to the effect that Chinese texts such as the *Jôgan Seiyô* (Chêng-kuan-kung-szu) and

Teihan (Ti-fan) were read and collated with each other. Copies of the *Teikan Seiyô* were made in Japanese script. In such Buddhist services as offerings to Shôtoku Taishi, the Monju Bosatsu and Kannon and lectures which were held in the *Jibutsudô* (Household Buddhist shrine) of the shogun's house, warriors would attend and receive an education through Buddhism. Buddhist liturgies were performed in the Jufukuji Temple, and right after the service a sermon was given in the *hôjô* (parsonage) of the temple where many warriors would come to sit and listen.

Opportunities for a broad pursuit of letters were available in the shogun's house through such experiences. There was no attempt to set up special schools for this purpose. The education that was available was not meant only for the shogun alone, but was also designed to give some education to warriors who had high status. On these occasions, literary men, scholars and famous priests were selected as teachers. It was characteristic of the warriors to receive education in their actual life rather than through specialized institutions.

Hitherto, most Japanese histories of education have indicated that the Kanazawa Bunko and the Ashikaga school were the only educational institutions and no others existed. Education in letters was considered scant and desolate. However, it is a problem whether or not even these institutions were at all representative of the education of the warrior families.

According to the *Hôjô Kudaiki*,[1] Akitoki (1248–1301), the son of Sanetoki, established the Kanezawa Bunko in the Shômyôji Temple. There he assembled Japanese and Chinese books. We are told that it began with his intention to make scholarship central, and it is said that "those who aspired to read and study the classics gathered there, both nobles and commoners, priests and laymen, and they pursued the study of literature". The library was evidently a centre for liberal education. The correspondence of Sadaaki indicates that the books of the library were lent and borrowed. Thus, it is clear that the *Bunko* was functioning as a

---

1 A chronology of the nine generations of the Hôjô family, covering the period 1183–1332, compiled in the *Zoku Gunsho-ruijû*.

library, and it became an institution for liberal education based on its books.

However, Shômyôji Temple was originally a temple of the Hôjô family where they first constructed a *jibutsudô*. When it became a temple, a library was also placed there and books collected. That means, the temple of a particular family, Hôjô, assumed at the same time a cultural function. Accordingly, it did not operate in a manner which we would call a school. We must interpret it as the central place of learning for their family where Sanetoki and Akitoki became intimate with scholarship.

The circumstances of the founding of the Ashikaga school are not clear. The founding legend which is most reliable states that it began when Ashikaga Yoshikane (? –1199) established his *gakumonjo* (study centre). We may now accept the connection of Yoshikane and the Ashikaga school because it is known that he established the Bannaji Temple of the Ashikaga family and that he had a great love of learning. From this it is believed that he established a *gakumonjo* there which became the Ashikaga school. Sometime later Uesugi Norizane (1411–1466) revived the Ashikaga school by organizing and donating books to it. After this time the school took a more modern form and was called the Ashikaga school.

Neither the Kanazawa Bunko, nor the Ashikaga school, which are called medieval schools, really had the form of a school. They were study centres established in association with the temples of the Hôjô or Ashikaga clans, and they did not exist apart from the life of the warrior families. They were not special institutions designed to provide education in letters to the warrior families, but were primarily for the use of the Hôjô and Ashikaga families or the upper strata of warrior families.

However, most warriors had a similar idea, and they made the temples they owned into centres for the education of their children. Originally there were children who lived in the temples as *chigosuihatsu* (long-haired novices) with the intention of becoming priests in the future. The children of the warriors joined them in the temples to receive an education in letters and became the companions of the child-monks. Here they spent

several years, but they did not aspire to become monks. After receiving
discipline in manners, spiritual training, writing and classical studies,
they would leave the temple. Examples of this feature of warrior education may be found in the passage of the *Gikeiki* entitled, "The story of
Ushiwaka entering the temple of Kurama". Ushiwaka ascended to
Mount Kurama at the age of seven. It is reported that all day long until
far into the night he read the *sutras* and practised writing. The *Tale of
Soga* also relates how Hakoô laboured in the temple until he was seventeen years old. Following the general pattern of entering the temple,
children usually began at the age of ten and resided there for about four
or five years. This was regarded as sufficient time to complete a general
education. The *Jikyôkun* (Discipline of Children) states:

"Thus, we thought that if he would have stayed at the temple for four
or five years, he might show some sign of intelligence. However, he
could not remain even three years and retreated to his native place..."

From this statement we may conjecture that a period of four or five
years was expected. There is also a passage in the *Sekyôshô* entitled "The
liturgical manner of child novitiates." This text gives an outline of a
day's work from which we can learn how the children lived in the
monasteries. According to the accounts, the children read the *sutras* in the
early morning. Until noon they practised penmanship. During the
afternoon they read stories, and various books. From about four o'clock
they had recreation in the various arts. Japanese poetry, stories, playing
the traverse flute, flute *à bec* and other music took up the evening time.

Reading of *sutras* and other books and practice of penmanship represent
the most basic aspects of education in the temples for the warrior children. For this practice of composition a variety of textbooks came to be
employed and provided patterns for letter writing, everyday vocabulary
necessary in the warrior's life, and material for reading which instilled
basic attitudes and ideas supporting the warrior way of life. Among these
texts were the *ôraibon* which were collections of correspondence to be
used as models. The letters deal with everyday affairs and were a good
basis for composition and reading.

The oldest of these texts is the *Meigô Ôrai* and it is reputed to have been composed by Fujiwara no Akihira (989–1066). More than two hundred and ten letters were assembled in it, and through its use as a composition book students could become well-versed in correspondence. The *Shin Sarugôki* is also said to have been a textbook written by Akihira. It contains terms covering the principal areas of life which were required in their activities.

The fact that these early textbooks were compiled entirely from materials associated with the life of the warrior families demonstrates again that warrior education was distinguished by its close connection to their way of life.

Many *ôraibon* were produced during the warrior age, and they may be classified into various types. There were those which preserved their original form as collections of letters. Among these are the *Kirei Mondô* (Questions and Answers on Court Manners), *Jûnigetsu Ôrai* (Twelve Months Correspondence), *Shin Jûnigetsu Ôrai* (New Twelve Months Correspondence). The latter collection served principally to teach the form and method of letter writing by giving examples of each month's exchanges of letters.

A second type of collection were those giving the words and phrases employed in letters. Works of this type are the *Shinrei Ôrai* (New Manner Correspondence), *Zappitsu Ôrai* (Miscellaneous Correspondence) and the *Sekiso Ôrai* (Common Correspondence). These texts do not take the form of letters, but are texts where one receives drill in letter writing through mastering the vocabulary for letter writing. Other kinds of *ôraibon* took the form of letters, but they interwove with them knowledge relating to the way of life revealed in the letters. As letters they are very unnatural, but as textbooks they fulfilled the function of encyclopedias. Works in this class are *Sammitsu Ôrai*, *Iseiteikin Ôrai*, *Teikin Ôrai*, and the *Yûgaku Ôrai*. From these books one could learn the everyday vocabulary related to various occupations, and fundamental concepts could also be attained. The *Shinsen Ruijû Ôrai* went beyond these texts in adding a glossary to the collections of letters, and it departed from the letter form.

After the beginning of the Edo period in Japan the various types of *ôraibon* were classified, and the texts were widely used for education in composition and penmanship. Education in letters in warrior families was frequently limited to the scope of this material.

The *ôraibon* were also used as reading material, and some works were composed with that end in view. Such works are the *Dôjikyô* (Children's Precepts), *Jitsugokyô* (Collection of Maxims), and the *Sanjikyô* (Three Character Epigrams). These texts gave a description of the life discipline and came to have the force of a kind of scripture for children because of the stress on fundamental attitudes in daily life. Books of family precepts *(kakun)* also held a similar position though they were first originally composed to instruct heirs of the family. They came to be widely used as textbooks as they gave general precepts governing everyday life.

On a more advanced level the *shikimoku* (codes and regulations) were adopted as reading material. An outstanding text of this type was the *Jôei Shikimoku* (Codes and Regulations of the Jôei period, 1232). Legal documents of the warriors were employed as examples for reading. On a much more advanced level Buddhist texts such as the *Hokekyô (Saddharma—Pundarika)* and *Kannonkyô (Avalokites Vara Sutra)* were widely read. While not all of these texts were used by the children of the warrior families, they do constitute the principal content of their reading material. Later works of exegesis on Confucian texts were also included, but these were probably used also by a limited number of people.

Finally we may note that the warrior's education was strikingly different from that of the aristocrat. It also differed from that which we will find in the Edo period. Its most conspicuous feature was that it had close connection to his way of life and lacked formal institutions. The warriors had a very practical philosophy of education, which did not allow them to separate their children from their way of life as warriors by entrusting them to educational institutions.

CHAPTER IV

Education in the Tokugawa Period

Education of the Warriors

In the Tokugawa period, Japanese society was, as before, a warrior society. Consequently, education was centred on the training of warriors. Nevertheless, the education of the warriors or samurai in the Edo period was considerably different from that of the medieval warriors. The organization of the later warrior society took shape when the Tokugawa clan transferred the shogunate to Edo (modern Tokyo), and made it the political capital. Also the *han* (clans) in the provinces were established and governed by the local lords.

After this kind of organization was established the city of Edo prospered as the political centre of Japan. Towns, called *jōkamachi* were founded as the seats of clan governments. Within these domains various classes such as warriors, farmers, artisans and merchants earned their living. The warriors held the highest position in the society, and they lived in the castle-towns or the most important towns in the domain of their lord. The other occupations were carried out in each town and village of the domain. The warriors built mansions in the castle-towns and lived peacefully for 270 years.

In the course of time the original character of life of the warriors, such as archery, horsemanship and warfare was lost. Most striking was the fact that the primary aim of life, i.e. warfare and fighting, disappeared. Warrior families no longer gained reputation and honour on the battlefield through military skills. They lived in a stable, feudal organization, with high status and ruling power among the people of their domains. As their mode of existence was transformed with the changing society, so the content of their education changed.

Not only the education of samurai changed in the Edo period, but the townspeople also gave a more organized education to their children. The merchants *(chōnin)*, especially, attained considerable economic power in that society, and they had great influence in the society. As a result, after the onset of the Tokugawa age, the education of the townspeople flourished and took a different pattern of organization from that of the warriors. We must distinguish in this period between the education of the warrior class of samurai who held a high rank in the society and the education of the common people who served under them. But these common people gradually came to have real power and influence in the society.

During Tokugawa times the warrior families attempted to give education in both military arts and letters. They had the same objective as the earlier medieval warriors. They differed from them in providing schools to educate their children in letters and military arts where the earlier warriors did not. Since the later warriors did not have the battlefield as the main object of their education as did the earlier warriors, the basic methods of education of their children were transformed. The warriors of the Tokugawa period also differed from the medieval warriors in not requiring their children to enter temples and undergo religious practices with the monks.

In order for the warriors of the Tokugawa period to educate their children, they set up schools. Such schools were not established all at once in either Edo or in the provinces where the *han* were located. In the beginning those among the daimyo (local lords), who were earnest in scholarship in the regional *han* and in Edo, invited scholars to give lectures and required the warriors of important offices to attend and listen. From these activities schools were gradually formed. In the beginning of the period there were few schools, but from about the middle of the era we can observe the establishment of schools in the large *han*. They increased as the era drew to a close. The greater part of the *han* provided schools in the castle-towns or other towns in the domains, and it was common for their children to commute to school to pursue their studies.

The largest of the schools for warrior families in Tokugawa times was the school set up in Edo for the shogunate. Tokugawa Ieyasu (1542–1616) had a great interest in Confucianism, and he sponsored and attended lectures in Confucian studies. He promoted Hayashi Razan (1583–1657) as the main lecturer. Meanwhile, he built a private school for the Hayashi family at Shinobugaoka. Here the members of the Hayashi family studied and lectured on Confucianism under the special protection of the shogunate. In the time of Iemitsu (1604–1651), the third Shogun, a school building was constructed for the Hayashi family at Shinobugaoka which was called Kôbunkan. It had a special relation to the shogunate.

Tsunayoshi (1646–1709), the fifth Shogun, established the shogunate school at Shôheizaka in Yushima, and he erected the sacred temple dedicated to Confucius. Scholars of the Hayashi family were appointed as presidents (*gakutô*) who gave lectures on Confucianism. Tsunayoshi himself enjoyed Confucian studies and not only the Hayashi family, but the Shogun himself lectured on the *Lun yu*. The retainers of the Shogun had to attend these lectures and eventually the Shôheizaka Academy became a school administered by the shogunate and gradually became the pattern for schools established by the warrior families in each feudal clan.

The shogunate made Confucian studies central in its curriculum. The Academy was eventually broadened, and its lecturers were not only drawn from the Hayashi family, but other Confucian scholars were hired. Since the majority of scholars in the *han* schools throughout the country had studied in the Shôheizaka Academy, this was regarded as the main school for the whole nation.

As the Shôheizaka Academy developed, dormitories were provided within its campus. The method was adopted of giving the students examinations to indicate the progress of their scholarship. In addition to this institution, the shogunate built other schools on a small scale where

Confucian scholars gave lectures. Sometimes schools were set up in areas held directly by the shogunate throughout the country. For example there were the Chôheikan Academy in Kôfu and the Academy in Nikkô for warrior children in these regions.

In addition to the school for Confucian studies at Shôheizaka in Edo, the shogunate set up other schools such as the Wagaku-kôdanjo or seminar for Japanese studies in 1793. Here lectures and investigations were made concerning ancient Japanese classics. In order to teach Japanese and Chinese medicine, the Igakkan or medical institute was formed in 1791 for the training of doctors. At the end of the shogunate the Kaiseijo or new academy was set up in 1863 to teach Western science and languages. Here many students enrolled for studies in the scholarship of the new era. Also the Kôbusho or military academy was organized in 1856 to teach Western artillery, strategy and navigation, as well as other military arts of the modern era. The schools of the shogunate in Edo pursued a broad range of scholarship covering the fields of Confucianism, national classics, Japanese and Chinese medicine, Western medicine and military sciences, modern science and Western languages. Since each of these schools was administered by the shogunate in Edo as a special college, it may be considered that a combined university existed in Edo in that period.

In each province in the nation, the *han* provided schools for their retainers. A representative school was the clan school of the castle-town. These schools were under the administration of the local clan families and designed for their children. Expenses were paid from each local *han* government. The schools were frequently built near the castle so it was easy to commute. However, there were differences in the scale of schools depending on the size of the clan and its strength. Schools of the greater clans had larger campuses, and they possessed school gates, buildings, dormitories, Confucian chapels and places for the practice of the military arts. They were imposing in appearance.

In addition to the schools set up in the castle-towns, other schools were organized in the important towns of the domain on a smaller scale for the warriors of those regions. In some cases, they also became places where lectures were given to those of the common people who desired to learn. Schools established by the clans in their towns were called *gôgaku* or local provincial schools.

The process of the establishment of the clan schools and the local schools resembled in great measure that leading to the formation of the shogunate schools in Edo. At first the local lords and their vassals were interested in Confucianism and invited scholars to lecture. From this schools evolved. In the greater clans such schools were set up from about the beginning of the Edo period, and from the middle of the era the lesser clans followed the same pattern. About the end of the Tokugawa era, almost all clans had established schools where their children could pursue scholarship and military arts. As a result, the clan schools became an important educational institution. At least one school for warrior families existed, administered by the clan head, in every one of the 170 or more clans throughout the nation. The castle-town schools reached 250 or 260 in number. Here the warriors who governed and led the Edo society received their formal education.

The *han* or clan schools were set up and administered independently according to the situation in each area. As a result, there was no uniform system created for the whole nation. Each *han* determined for itself at what age an individual could enter the school and how long he had to study there. It was frequently the case that students began school at the age of 7 or 8 years and graduated at 15 to 20 years of age after completing the specified course. Some clans had their students enter school at 15 years of age. In such cases the student would commute to a private school until he was 15 in order to receive a basic education. After entering the clan school, he pursued an advanced course of study. There were also instances where one had to attend school even after reaching 30 years of age. Accordingly, institutions for the adult education of the clan warriors were developed. The clan schools differed strikingly from present-day schools in requirements for entering and completing the school course. The reason for this was that there was no special system of clan schools and no necessity for liaison between the schools.

The purpose of the clan schools as in earlier times was to provide education in letters and the military arts for warriors. The clan schools which devoted great effort to education in letters concentrated on Chinese studies. Chinese studies refers to education based completely on the ancient Chinese classics. The content of such study was divided into four parts, namely, the classics, history, poetry and prose.

The study of the classics employed Chinese texts and commentaries. These commentaries were made in Japan in order to teach the principles of Confucianism. Chinese historical texts were used for the study of history, while the poetic section of the classics provided material for the study of poetry. Students not only studied the Chinese poems themselves, but they composed poems in Chinese characters. Superior examples of Chinese writing were used as models in the study of prose, and the students wrote their own compositions in Chinese.

Since these four studies were universally regarded as indispensable for a clan warrior, a great number of Confucian scholars as well as those who excelled in poetry and prose were invited to lecture at the clan schools. At that time there were factions among the Confucian scholars, but the Shôheizaka Academy was regarded as the centre for the study of Chu Hsi, the leading Chinese Confucian school. Since the Hayashi family of Confucian scholars belonged to the Chu Hsi school and for several generations they were most prominent in the education of the clan children, most Confucian scholars in the clan schools were also followers of Chu Hsi. In some clan schools, however, some pursued the study of the Wang Yang Ming school. Hence, the study of Chu Hsi was not entirely universal throughout the nation.

In addition to the study of Chinese classics, other areas of scholarship such as medicine, national classics and Western studies were also considered part of a liberal education. The study of medicine was important for providing doctors for the clans. Since it was a specialized field not open to the general student, special schools were set up within the clan school for training doctors. The national classics consisted of study based on the Japanese classical texts from which the students learned about Japanese culture and tradition. This study was carried on parallel with study of the Chinese classics.

The introduction of the study of national classics into the scholarship of the clan schools was a later development. From the time of the decline of the shogunate, the study of the national classics came to be regarded as increasingly important, and the study was gradually adopted in the clan schools. However, not every school gave attention to this study.

Western studies included modern European languages and advanced modern scholarship of the West. At first, Western studies were based on the mastering of the Dutch language, but at the end of the Tokugawa shogunate, French and English were increasingly studied. The study of the natural sciences flourished greatly. Through such studies the shogunate gradually became familiar with affairs in the various Western nations. As the people were greatly interested in these matters, Western studies began to draw more attention in the clan schools and great strides were made in all areas.

Since the study of Chinese classics was central to the curriculum of the clan school, methods of study in this area were better organized. At first, children began the study of Chinese with the method termed *sodoku* which was a method of reciting the classical text without understanding the content. Students memorized the text by reading after the teacher. The texts used in this method of recitation were the *Hsiao-hsue (Shôgaku)* and *Hsiao Ching (Kôkyô* or Book of Filial Piety). After the student achieved a degree of skill in reciting such Chinese classics as *Shisho-gokyô* (the Four Books and Five Classics), he attended the lecture meetings.

Through lectures the meaning of the sentences they had memorized recited came to be understood. The most important method for learning the classics was to attend such lectures while in the clan school. Confucian scholars made their own interpretations, while they also used traditional Japanese and foreign interpretations and theories concerning the classics. Most study time was employed in this fashion. In order to deepen their understanding, methods such as *kaidoku* and *rinkô* were used. *Kaidoku* refers to the meetings in which the students gathered in a group to read the texts together. *Rinkô* refers to the method in which students gathered and each made his own interpretation of the texts based on the thought and commentaries of other Confucianists. The students would express their opinions in turn and discuss them together. Through attending meetings where one or the other procedure was followed (called *sodoku-seki, kaidoku-seki,* and *rinkô-seki,* respectively), the student could indicate his scholarly achievement as the teacher observed and evaluated his learning.

The military aspect of the warrior's training was also an important part of the clan school. While pursuing a liberal education, he also had to learn to be a warrior. A training hall for the martial arts was provided separately from the liberal arts. The warrior, as in earlier times, trained with weapons in order to become skillful in archery, horsemanship, swordsmanship, spearmanship and swimming. Military science became a part of the course, and military scientists lectured on the military books *(heisho)*. The teachers organized the content of the texts under various topics such as strategy or fortifications according to their respective scholarly factions. The students learned the conduct of warfare through the interpretation of these texts.

When the young men completed their course of study, they returned home and became the companions of the warrior children in the towns. From such companions the children received both education and enjoyment. The companions formed themselves into groups and had names as "such and such" *kumi,* "such and such" *ren,* or "such and such" *renchû.* The oldest individual in the group became the leader. The names of such bands differed according to the clan, and in the Satsuma clan, for example, they were called *gôjyô.* Such organizations of warrior children were considered important educational institutions by the clans. The companions had a meeting hall in the town where they gathered every day, and studied Chinese literature with the help of more accomplished individuals through the method of *sodoku* recitation. Sometimes they practised military arts or used games and entertainments to broaden their learning. While these extracurricular activities were not a part of formal educations they were an important aspect of the total education of the warriors.

The warrior tradition of medieval Japan persisted in the society of the Tokugawa period and the education of the children in such families was severe. Through such strict drill and training which was very different from that of the common people, the warrior's children were expected to manifest their superiority to the farmers, artisans and merchants.

They received particularly severe training in discrete behaviour as well as in seating manners and etiquette, according to their seniority in the family. Etiquette was systematized and there were families such as the Ogasawara who made it their speciality to instruct in such procedures. The standards of etiquette and ceremony which they established became the foundation for discipline in the warrior's way of life. Most important and necessary in the warrior's life were the strict manners and etiquette required in the performance of military arts and in the seating manners in the mansions of the shogun and daimyo on ceremonial occasions.

In the Edo period the house precepts were also regarded as important in the warrior's education. Many of the house rules of the warrior families have been preserved until today. The way of thinking does not differ from what is found in the medieval period when these rules provided the standards and basic principles for the control of the family. The family life of the warrior was viewed as an important place of education as he practised the rules forming his way of life and governed his family by them.

Education of the Townspeople

When the townspeople came to have more social influence during the Tokugawa period, they also developed a characteristic system of education for their children. Since the way of life of these people differed considerably from that of the nobility or warriors, the education they required also differed. For example, we read in the *Nippon Eitaigura:*[1]

---

1 The title of this book which was written by Ihara Saikaku in 1688 is translated differently by three translators: *The Way to Wealth* (Soji Mizuno), *The Japanese Family Storehouse* (G. W. Sargent), *The Eternal Storehouse of Japan* (Ivan Morris).

The art of poetry is for the nobles; that of archery and horsemanship is for the warriors. But the townsmen *(chônin)* should excel in computation and learn to keep book punctually.

In this statement the townspeople expressed the special character of their way of life by comparing it with the poetry writing of the nobility and the military arts of the warrior.

The townspeople believed that they found their place in life by means of computation in business, and they sought to prosper their families by acquiring money and property through skill in business. Such an outlook is expressed in the *Seken Musuko Katagi*:[1]

In general, merchants should pay attention day and night to every detail in order to earn more money.

The *Nebikino-kadomatsu*[2] relates:

The samurai become warriors because their parents raise them in the way of warriors, while merchants become merchants because their their parents instruct them in business affairs. The warriors reject profit and seek fame, while the merchants reject fame and take profit. Piling up riches is the way of a merchant.

This text strikingly portrays the difference in outlook on life of the warriors and the merchants.

In order to make profit and prosper one's family by accumulating money and property, it was necessary that the merchant give special attention and diligent effort to whatever job he had to do. This sentiment is clearly expressed in the *Chôka Shikimoku Bungen Dama no Ishizue*:[3]

When one is attentive, the gods of happiness will protect him even though he does not pray. His family will prosper so that his shop will become like a market place. Without avariciously asserting himself to gain silver, his house will be filled with treasures and gold.

It was the generally accepted principle of the time that all who entered business desired wealth and that they devoted themselves to that end day

---

1 *The General Way of the Life of Sons.*
2 *The Lucky New Year Pine,* a play written by Chikamatsu Monzaemon.
3 *The Basic Principles of the Rules and Rights of Townsmen.*

and night. In order to develop as a merchant or to associate with them, one had to work hard at his business and give it care and undivided attention. Whether or not one would prosper as a merchant depended on one's individual skill. One's house would flourish through single-minded labour or become impoverished through slackness.

The *Seken Musuko Katagi* also states:

> The study of the young master which does not relate to money-making is a cause of the decline of his house. He learns such things as morality, but some study of the abacus would help the house... Give up reading literature and think of book-keeping.

Here we see that the merchants did not feel that learning such things as Confucianism would bring any profit, and they did not regard them as necessary. Instead, they demanded that a person should be more skillful in computation and book-keeping.

In order for the townspeople and merchants to educate their children in these skills, they taught them reading, writing and the use of the abacus. These were the foundation of education. Such education, however, was given outside the home of the merchant by teachers to whom the children were sent. The fundamental form of education developed by the merchants in the Tokugawa period was the *terakoya* which was a private, elementary school originally set up in temples for the common people.

As the term *terakoya* indicates, such schools developed in the Buddhist temples *(tera)*. Actually they originated before the Tokugawa period. As we have seen earlier, the warriors had employed temples in the education of their children, and at about the close of the Muromachi era (1336–1573) the common people also used the temples to educate their children in a manner similar to the warriors. In the Tokugawa period conspicuous progress in the development of these institutions took place. The *terakoya* evolved into institutions for general education apart from the temples as independent schools. The term *terakoya* as used by historians today refers to these new independent schools. In the same period, new terms were used also to describe various functions in education such as *tenarai shishô* or teacher of penmanship, and *hitsudô shinan* or professor of calligraphy.

The *terakoya* was firmly established from about the time of Kyôhô
(1716–1735). A description is given in the *Keizairoku*[1] of Dazai Shundai
(1680–1747):

> At present, children over seven or eight years of age gather at the
> houses of instructors who teach writing, the reading of such materials
> as *Imagawa-jô,*[2] *Teikin Shikimoku*[3] concerning manners and customs,
> and the use of multiplication tables.

As to the number of teachers engaged in instruction, the *Kenzan Hisaku*[4]
indicates that there were more than 800 in Edo.

To these 800 *terakoya* the private citizens voluntarily sent their children
to be taught. The teachers might be originally warriors, merchants or
monks, shinto priests and even doctors. In most cases the teacher was
responsible for twenty or thirty students who ranged in age from six or
seven years to about eleven. The students generally attended the school
for about three or four years. They gathered everyday at eight a.m. and
studied until three p.m. Most of the time was spent in penmanship which
led to the comment in the *Ukiyoburo*:[5]

> Many children, with their faces, hands and legs stained with ink, look
> like negroes. With their eyes alone shining, they came in (the bath)
> with a lot of noise. It was about the eighth hour (ten o'clock).

The education of the *terakoya* consisted largely in mixing the *sumi* ink
in the morning and being taught penmanship by the teacher throughout
the day. Frequently *tenaraibon* or books of penmanship were used. The
content of such books included material based on the way of life of merchants. The instruction began with the practice of the *iroha* or Japanese
syllabary, *hôgaku* (names of places and directions), and computation.
After learning and memorizing fundamental characters, the students
progressed to the use of such texts as the *Edo Hôgaku* which provided
geographical names of Edo arranged in rhyme for memorizing, *Shôbai*

---

1 *On Economics.*
2 The precepts of Imagawa Family written by Imagawa Sadayo (1325-1420).
3 The Family Precepts of the late Muromachi period; the author unknown.
4 The Correspondence of Muro Kyûsô written in 1711-31.
5 *The Bathhouse of the Floating World* by Shikitei Samba (1776-1822).

Ôrai which contained material for business correspondence, *Shôsoku Ôrai* composed of materials for general correspondence, *Kojôzoroe* which were collections of famous letters, *Teikin Ôrai* relating to family precepts, *Nagashira* giving lists of family names, *Sommei* or lists of villages and the *Kunizukushi* or lists of provinces. These texts served as models both for writing and for learning materials useful in business. The most common materials used in the *terakoya* are given in the *Terakoya Monogatari*:[1]

Nagashira, Edo Hôgaku, Sommei, and *Shôbai Ôrai*—that's enough!

The textbooks of penmanship were of various types generally called *ôraimono* (correspondence). They were selected and based on the scope of life of the child of a townsman. From such materials the children learned details of the world about them while learning to write. For example, the *Nagashira* gave them information on the family names commonly seen around them. The *Sommei, Gummei* and *Kunizukushi* gave practice in writing the names of villages, counties and provinces. The collections of letters taught them vocabulary and forms of writing. The *Edo Hôgaku* was a directory of Edo. Works like the *Miyakôji* relating the roads to the capital, and *Mairimono,* which was a pilgrim's guidebook, gave instruction in geography. The *Kojôzoroe* provided information for historical study. For education in the commercial way of life the *Shôbai Ôrai* and *Shôsoku Ôrai* were particularly useful. As a result, the textbooks of penmanship were compiled with a view to providing in a co-ordinated fashion all kinds of information which the town children would need for their daily lives. While they practised writing, they gained the knowledge and words necessary to their way of life as businessmen. Naturally, this mode of teaching calligraphy differed from the study of calligraphy in present-day schools. The reason that they studied calligraphy the whole day can be understood from the fact that it was co-ordinated with practical content.

In addition to the fact that they were used for practice in calligraphy,

---

1 *Story of the Temple School.*

the penmanship texts, such as *Jitsugokyô*[1], *Dôjikyô*,[2] *Sanjikyô*,[3] *Onna Daigaku*,[4] *Onna Imagawa*,[5] and *Onna Shisho*[6] were also used for reading. In some cases, instruction was also given to more advanced students in reading the Chinese classics.[7] The content of these books gave instruction in living and provided the standards which the townspeople wished their children to learn. Thus, in the education of the *terakoya* the child received discipline and training in his attitude towards life.

Training in the abacus was also an important feature of the education in the *terakoya*. Students began with exercises in simple addition and subtraction on the *soroban* (abacus). They then progressed to multiplication and division and learned to estimate prices. The *Jingôki*,[8] *Kaisanki*,[9] and *Nichiyô Sampôsho* were popular as mathematical texts in teaching the elements of the abacus.

Skill in learning the abacus was, of course, indispensable for the business townspeople. However, only the first steps were taught in the *terakoya*. One would learn the abacus more freely and thoroughly after he left the school and entered into a business firm as an apprentice. It was the usual procedure for students to serve in a business house to learn their duties upon completion of studies in the *terakoya*. The apprentices learned the business by going into the head office of a business or a client's office. Sometimes he lived until he was an adult in a merchant's house where he learned the transactions of the business. When the children of the towns-

---

1 A textbook for elementary education in Japan used for over 700 years.

2 A textbook for *terakoya* education edited in the Muromachi period. The author unknown.

3 A textbook for children written in Chinese characters; each of three letters were put in rhyme.

4 A book of ethics for women written by Kaibara Ekiken (1630-1714) for his wife.

5 Women's morals written by Sawada Kichi in 1700.

6 Women's morals compiled by Wang Tsing Sheng and rearranged in Japanese in about 1850.

7 *Ssi shu* (namely, *Ta hsueh*, *Chung Yung*, *Lun yu*, *Meng tze*) and *Wu ching* (namely, *I ching*, *Shih chi*, *Li chi*, *Chun ch'iu tsuo shih ch'uan*)

8 Written by Yoshida Mitsuyoshi (d. 1672), published in 1727.

9 Written by Yamada Hikozaemon in 1659.

people completed their apprenticeships they usually inherited the family business of their parents or set up their own shops.

In order to become an apprentice, a child would leave his own home about the age of ten and live in the house of a merchant. He was first treated as a shop boy *(detchi)* and did the cleaning or ran errands. As he became older he ran errands in the neighbourhood. At the age of fifteen or sixteen when he was considered half grown, he was given the job of keeping stores and taking baggage in and out besides his various other duties. He might also keep books and receive or disburse money. At the age of eighteen or nineteen the individual might become a clerk *(tedai)*, and following the instructions of his supervisor *(bantô)* would be busy laying in stock and selling. During this time he might engage in business speculation on his own and become skilled in business transactions. Thus, he was permitted to make deals with customers in the shop, to take care of the account books and to represent his employer. He was acquainted with most business affairs by the age of twenty-five and after some service of gratitude, he would return home or open a shop. Sometimes he continued in the shop and later became a manager.

It was not at all unusual during this time for the children of the towns-people to work extremely hard. For it was through such diligent labour that they could establish themselves as heads of excellent firms. They also could attain some understanding of the feelings of a servant, as well as cultivate necessary skills in the strategy and tactics of business. It is to be noted that there were many cases where the family property and wealth were squandered by individuals who did not undergo the period of apprenticeship, but merely stayed at home and inherited their parents' businesses. The *Ukiyoburo* states:

It is very difficult for us to take care of our Master (heir). Since he is the only son, he has been brought up too indulgently in all affairs, and he was not sent out for apprenticeship. Now they regret it. Although one may be intelligent at home, he is useless unless he learns something of the world outside. Frequently he may ignore the way of making money and become a prodigal.

Also:

> One should learn to live in homes other than his own. Otherwise, one
> is never capable of thinking of another's way of life. For example,
> when one hires a servant, he will not understand the servant's suffering
> unless he has himself experienced it before.

According to these passages, the merchant children needed the experience of apprenticeship in order to learn the true ways of business. It
was thought that, if, because of the excessive tenderness of the parents,
an individual stayed at home and was not sent for apprenticeship, he
could never become a superior merchant.

The merchants pursued the same mode of education for their daughters as for their sons. In such cases a daughter would become a maid in a
great house when she became fourteen or fifteen years old. This was
called *oyashiki bôkô* or house-maid service. There were also examples of
girls who entered service at six years of age accompanied by a nurse.
Sometimes daughters of a great merchant family would enter the service
of a daimyo. In such cases they would be accompanied by a servant.
During their period of labour, they would receive drill in every phase of
domestic life. They would learn the various arts including the rules of
etiquette and manners, polite use of words, reading, writing, Japanese
poetry, music and dancing. If it was a particularly large mansion, the
girls were given a high degree of education as the companion of the
daughter of the house, or the matron and wife of the house. Also the
daughters of merchants who returned home from such service received
lessons in the *samisen* and other music. In order to learn to sew, she would
commute to a dressmaker's shop. The method of educating the daughters
of merchants is clearly expressed in a story concerning a merchant's wife
in the *Ukiyoburo*:

> Housemaid service is important. One learns good manners without
> being taught. So long as a girl lives with her parents, even the severest
> words cannot correct her bad manners. Once she is sent to a mansion
> of a lord, her manners gradually improve in one way or another.

The basis of the merchant's daily life was the plain moral teachings of
the sages. To give instructions in these teachings special institutions called

kyôyujo, nikkôjo and *shingakusha* were set up in each area. The Senkyô-
kan, established in Kyoto to give lectures on morality, held lectures or
gave interpretations of the classics each month in the evening on the first,
sixth, eleventh, sixteenth, twenty-first and twenty-sixth days. On the
evenings of the third, eighth, thirteenth, eighteenth, twenty-third and
twenty-eighth days, *shingaku dôwa,* that is, lectures in *shingaku* teaching
were given. At the Yushima Seidô, a Confucian temple, daily lectures on
Confucian doctrine were begun in 1717. Popular lectures and studies of
the classics were provided also for lower class warriors and merchants.

The Shingakusha begun by Ishida Baigan in Kyoto was an institution
particularly designed for merchants to teach them the "learning of the
mind" *(shingaku)* as a practical ethic. It attained a wide influence in
Tokugawa society. Baigan states in his text *Tohimondô* (Questions and
Answers on City and Country):

   What I teach is the life of the merchants. I do not teach anything about
   the way of warriors, farmers or artisans.

Restricting himself thus to the merchant class, he describes his doctrine
in the *Kyûô-dôwa:*

   The way of saints cannot be understood at all by maids and children so
   long as the doctrine is incomprehensible. *Shingaku-dôwa* is not originally designed for intellectuals. It was the will of my teacher to propa-
   gate the way of saints among farmers and merchants who have little
   time to spare in reading because of their daily work. I try my best to
   use simple language and make use of examples and illustrations. I
   integrate everything reasonable whether it is from Shinto religion or
   Buddhism.

Baigan taught in simple words the way of life and thinking for merchants. Furthermore, he caused them to strive to learn the psychology of
people, so that one might see his own true nature. For this they had to
learn the distinctive rules of discipline of the *shingaku* teaching. The teaching flourished widely among the merchants because its moral teaching
was in close touch with their lives. The common people gathered in the
Shingakusha. Nakazawa Dôji describes one of these institutions called
the Sanzensha during the Kansei period (1789–1800):

The construction of the assembly hall of the Sanzensha of this locality has recently been completed and lectures begun on the twenty-third of this month. The audience was unexpectedly large. On the first day there were about five or six hundred attending. On the third day the audience increased to thirteen hundred, and about two hundred people were refused entrance.

These institutions flourished and the education which the townspeople received was considerable. It must be remembered that they were created by the townspeople themselves to provide a moral education.

From our study thus far of the Tokugawa period we have seen that the warriors provided special schools for their children, and the common people established separate schools called *terakoya* to give instruction in calligraphy and the knowledge necessary for a merchant. While some of these schools were begun at the beginning of the Edo period, they increased as the period developed. At the end of the shogunate, they were conspicuously numerous. Although there were about 270 provincial schools set up for warriors throughout the country, and in the various regions regional schools were established, the popular *terakoya* schools were small, private establishments and their number cannot be accurately determined. In any case, there were a great many schools both for warriors and common people, numbering in the hundreds.

After the end of the shogunate and in the time of the Meiji Restoration, such schools for common people had come to be set up in every town and village. In the Meiji period the *terakoya* were transformed into elementary schools *(shôgakkô)*. At that time, three or four local *terakoya* would be amalgamated into the village school. These *terakoya,* perhaps numbering above 40,000, and the existing warrior schools became the basis for the development of the modern school in the Meiji era.

CHAPTER V

The Establishment and Progress of
Modern Schools After the Meiji Restoration

The warrior society which had existed for many generations in Japan came to an end with the Meiji Restoration. The whole nation was unified and ruled by a newly formed government and the shogunate and clan institutions were abolished. As a result of this change, there was also a great reformation in education. The earlier educational concepts were transformed, and the school system and educational policies became radically new.

In the Edo period both the shogunate and the several clans had established and administered their own respective schools. There was no co-ordination between them, because the feudal system did not permit nation-wide educational planning. The common people provided small, private popular schools for their children to study reading, writing and the use of the abacus. While the schools for the common people were encouraged by the shogunate and clans, they did not try to reorganize them into an official educational system of the people.

In the Meiji period, the shogunate collapsed. The various clans were abolished as a result of the unification of the country. With these changes the warrior and popular schools were reorganized under a new educational policy. The government held to the ideal of the equality of the four classes of society—warriors, peasants, artisans, and merchants—and did not distinguish between the children of warriors or commoners. They made it their clear policy to establish an educational system in which all classes were regarded as citizens. In order to develop Japan as a modern nation, the leaders believed that they had to construct a system of national education so that individual citizens could develop their respective abilities sufficiently. Immediately after the Meiji Restoration the national leaders desired to make as rapid a transition to a modern state as possible through the education of the citizenry, and in this way establish Japan as an independent nation.

In order to accomplish this goal, they thought that they must establish schools where the youth could learn the necessary knowledge and techniques of the new age. At that time they observed the school systems and conditions of education in the most advanced countries of Europe and America and there acquired knowledge of the methods and organization of national education. Investigation into Western education began after 1868. In 1870 a system of schools organized into three stages, elementary, secondary or middle and university, was set up. The fields of study in the university were divided into the five faculties of pedagogy, letters, law, science and medicine, following the structure of Western universities. In 1872 the *Gakusei* or Government Order of Education was proclaimed and defined in detail the school system. This proclamation made it possible to instrument a unified educational programme for the whole nation.

After the division of the stages of education into elementary, secondary and university, a system of school districts or wards was adopted. According to the plan that was formulated, the whole country was divided into 53,760 elementary school districts. In each district there was to be one elementary school. Likewise, there were to be 256 middle school districts with one school each and then eight university districts. In this educational proposal lay the future development of Japanese schools. Various types of elementary schools were planned, and besides the usual middle schools there were plans for commercial and agricultural schools on the secondary level. In addition, night schools were proposed for those students who had to work during the day. With respect to college education, there were medical, law and arts and crafts schools apart from the universities. These schools never existed previously in Japan. They indicate the positive intention on the part of the leaders to establish schools comparable to those of Europe and America.

When the Order was put forward, the government announced its fundamental educational policy and objectives. According to this policy, all citizens had to follow a way of life which would develop them educationally and thus promote industry and commerce.

The acquirement of knowledge and cultivation of talent are essential to a successful life. By education men learn to acquire property, practise learned professions, perform public services, and make themselves independent of the help of their fellow men. Schools are designed to provide this essential education. In their various capacities they are intended to supply to all classes of men the knowledge necessary for a successful life... Although schools have existed for many centuries in Japan, yet those that have been provided by the government have been confined to the military retainers and to the upper classes. For the lower classes of society, and for women, learning was regarded as beyond their ken, and, if acquired at all, was of a limited character. Even among the higher classes, the character of education was defective. Under the pretext of acquiring knowledge for the benefit of the state, much time was spent in the useless occupation of writing poetry and composing elegant maxims, instead of learning what would be for their own benefit or that of the state. Recently an improved educational system has been formed, and the methods of teaching remodelled. It is planned that henceforth education shall not be confined to a few, but shall be so diffued that there may not be a village with an ignorant family, nor a family with an ignorant member.

Since the schools were to be for the whole citizenry, a liberal system was created based on the equality of the four classes of the nation. Each person was to receive at least an elementary school education. Those with superior abilities among the graduates were permitted to proceed for further study in the middle school. Those selected from the middle school graduates could enter the universities for advanced study. The Government Order of Education of 1872 envisioned a school system with a single line of organization, replacing the double line (for the warrior and the people) which characterized education of the Edo period. This change constitutes the most important characteristic of education since Meiji. The principle of this liberated school system can be observed running through Japanese education to the present day.

The elementary schools were the first to be launched under the new school system. It was planned that after completing the elementary schools, the middle schools and universities could be arranged. But since these schools were also provided for in the Government Order of Education, some middle schools, professional schools and universities were also set up. However, the actual work of establishing the schools was concentrated in the elementary schools. This was the result of the belief that without completing the elementary schools, the first stage of education, they could not complete middle schools and institutions of higher education. This policy was not only important for the development of schools, but it had great significance for the modernization of Japanese life, culture and industry. If the policy of expanding school education through the founding of elementary schools had not been successful, the way of life and culture which can presently be seen among the Japanese people would probably not have been possible.

To undertake such a school system, it was thought necessary not merely to learn from the modern schools of the West, but to invite educators from the advanced Western countries as leaders in carrying out the new educational policies and plans. In the fifty or sixty years after putting the new educational system into force, the number of foreign teachers who worked in Japan increased greatly. Most of them worked as teachers in the colleges and professional schools and guided the students. At that time students were also dispatched overseas to study modern American and European science and techniques. Due to the expense, however, the number of overseas students was very limited. As time passed, it was generally recognized as more urgent for the sake of modernizing Japan to invite foreign teachers to Japan and to entrust the education of students to them. Therefore, the latter policy was adopted. Further, as an advisor in educational administration, the Ministry of Education invited the American, David Murray, to Japan in 1873. He remained in Japan for five years giving advice on the implementation of the educational code.

Murray struggled with the question of how to combine successfully the Western educational system with the actual conditions in Japan.

Under the new educational system a new curriculum was adopted and the educational methods were also reformed. Subjects which had not been taught before were instituted, and materials and tools for education were modernized. The methods for constructing a modernized curriculum were modelled after European and American schools, and necessary materials and tools for teaching were introduced from those countries.

Textbooks were also important. Those used in the elementary schools were mostly translations or adaptations of European and American books. Many texts using these materials were published. In the middle schools and above, foreign textbooks were at first imported, or they were published verbatim. Soon, however, in the middle schools and universities, students used translated textbooks or books written by Japanese. It is obvious that such texts performed a great work in publicizing Western culture and learning. Also tables and chairs which were originally European or American came to be produced by Japanese. Blackboards and wall maps were also necessary in the classroom. These were first produced in Japan as supplies for the elementary schools. In this fashion, modern education began to function in the 1880's. The people found this new form of education attractive as a kind of cultural enlightenment, and they gradually permitted their children to enter the new schools.

Thus, the schools of the Edo period had been reformed with the Western schools as the model, but over against this movement there was a demand from the time of the Meiji Restoration that education also be reorganized on the basis of the Japanese educational tradition. This was made clear in the *Kyôgaku Taishi* (Principles of Education) of 1879 which claimed the support of the will of the Emperor. This text criticized the tendencies in education after the Restoration and stressed the importance of moral education. It states:

> The core of education lies in the clear teaching of benevolence, responsibility, loyalty, fidelity and in mastering knowledge and the arts

so that one can serve the people. This is the basic principle given by our ancestors and national literature which is commonly accepted for the instruction of all, high or low. But recently there have been a great many people who value only knowledge and techniques which are simply the products of cultural enlightenment, and who do not keep their morals but destroy good manners and customs. This is the result of the fact that the first principle of the Restoration was to destroy old customs and seek for knowledge in the world. Although the advantages of Western culture were adopted and resulted in spectacular effects for the moment, once it leads to a tendency to neglect benevolence, responsibility, loyalty and fidelity and becomes merely a competition to introduce Western manners, there is fear that in the future no one will know responsibility between the Emperor and his subjects. This is not the true motive of education in our nation. Therefore, henceforth, we shall make clear the virtues of benevolence, responsibility, loyalty and fidelity based on the precepts of our ancestors. In the teaching of morality the Confucian morality will be primary. Men will furthermore respect faithfulness and good manners. After that, learning in each field should be promoted according to the ability of the person. Thus, both morals and knowledge will be attained. Centring on the principle of attaining righteousness, education will be provided throughout the land. In that way the independent spirit of our country shall never be disgraced in the world.

The Bureau of Education revised the educational principles according to this policy of promoting moral education in the elementary schools and the middle schools. *Shûshin* or moral cultivation was placed at the head of the curriculum. For this purpose they compiled the *Shôgaku Shûshin Kun* (Instructions for the Cultivation of Morality in Elementary Schools) under the guidance of Shigeki Nishimura (1828–1902). This textbook obviously reflected Oriental morality. Further they prohibited the use of all textbooks which did not conform to the spirit of the *Kyôgaku Taishi*. In 1882 the Imperial Household published the *Yôgaku Kôyô* (Principles in the Teaching of Children), and they recommended it as a textbook of morality. Since the teachers fulfilled an important function in the promotion of moral education, the Bureau of Education issued the *Shôgakkô Yôin Kokoroe* (Memorandum for Elementary School Teachers). It required teachers to make moral education primary. In this way they attempted to advance the national character of Japan by combining Western knowledge and techniques with Oriental morality.

The Government Order of Education of 1872 provided the first national educational system in Japan, but it was a theoretical scheme based on the Western European educational system. Consequently, many problems arose with the implementation of this policy. Hence, the government altered the school system to meet the real conditions in the *Kyôiku Rei* (Education Law) which was published in 1879 and the earlier code was abolished. This new educational policy left control and administration of the schools to the various localities, but because of that in some places the enrolment in the elementary schools decreased. Consequently, in the next year, 1880, they changed the Education Law and adopted a centrally controlled administrative policy. Later in 1885, when the government was reorganized and a cabinet instituted, Arinari Mori (1847–89) was appointed as the first minister of education. At that time it was expected that the constitution would be promulgated in 1889, Diet members would be determined by election, and the Diet would be convened in 1890.

The Education Minister Mori carried out a complete reform of the educational system in 1886, and he constructed the foundation for the Japanese school system which lasted for a comparatively long period of time thereafter. For this reform he formulated the Elementary School Act to set in order the elementary schools which were the basis of the national education system. He published the provisions concerning the middle schools, the Imperial Universities and normal schools for training of teachers. Thus, the modernization of the schools after 1872 came to a conclusion with the establishment of the provisions for the four types of schools.

At about this time the national policy of enriching and strengthening the country (*Fukoku Kyôhei*) was established. The thought of elevating Japan to a first class nation among the nations of the world was predominant, and the attempt was made to strengthen this programme by means of the newly created school system.

It was thought that as the modernization of such a nation progressed, the structure of a strong national education to make the country prosper would not be complete unless there was added also a reform in the substance of education which goes along with the external form of the system. The education minister thought that together with cultivating the knowledge and skills necessary for modern life, one must make efforts also in the education of the spirit through establishing the policy of moral education. However, there were at that time various viewpoints on how to carry out education in morals, and there were disputes over the establishment of that policy. It was asserted that the basic moral concept in the spiritual education of the people must be firmly determined through Imperial Rescript. The Prime Minister, Aritomo Yamagata, also, agreed with this, and the Director of the Legislative Bureau, Kowashi Inoue, was a central figure in drafting the Imperial Rescript Through the co-operation of the Confucian scholar, Nagazane Motoda, Imperial Rescript on Education was formulated and proclaimed on the September 30, 1890. This Rescript on Education was for many years thereafter respected as clarifying the fundamental policy of national education. Hundreds of exegetical texts were published concerning the Imperial Rescript. The whole text of the Rescript was included in textbooks and interpretations were added. On ceremonial days the principal would assemble the students and read the Rescript, so that the students might understand thoroughly its policy. The text of the Rescript follows:

Know ye, Our subjects: Our Imperial Ancestors have founded Our Empire on a basis broad and everlasting, and have deeply and firmly implanted virtue; Our subjects, ever united in loyalty and filial piety, have from generation to generation illustrated the beauty thereof. This is the glory of the fundamental character of Our Empire, and herein lies the source of Our education. Ye, Our subjects, be filial to your parents, affectionate to your brothers and sisters; as husbands and wives be harmonious, as friends true; bear yourselves in modesty and moderation; extend your benevolence to all; pursue learning and cultivate arts, and thereby develop intellectual faculties and perfect moral powers; furthermore advance public good and promote common interests; always respect the Constitution and observe the laws; should emergency arise, offer yourselves courageously to the State; and thus guard and maintain the prosperity of Our Imperial Throne coeval with heaven and earth. So shall ye not only be Our good and faithful subjects, but render illustrious the best traditions of your forefathers. The Way here set forth is indeed the teaching bequeathed by Our Imperial Ancestors, to be observed alike by Their Descendants and the subjects, infallible for all ages and true in all places. It is Our wish to lay it to heart in all reverence, in common with you, Our subjects, that we may all thus attain to the same virtue.

From about the year 1894 industrial production in Japan began to be modernized. Consequently, it became a problem as to what policies should be set up for technical education. The Education Minister, Kowashi Inoue, at that time endeavoured to reform the educational system in view of business needs and particularly with progress in industrialization in mind. He also sought to found new schools. Later, complete reconstruction of the educational system was carried out, and within several years after 1899, the modern schools of Japan were completely organized. For about forty years after this, national education progressed according to the system set up at this time. The elementary schools were divided into "common" and "higher", each four years. Those who completed six years of primary education were permitted to enter middle school. The middle schools were designated as middle school for boys, higher girls' school, business schools, and continuation schools for workers in industry. For higher education there were colleges and the Imperial Universities. Various types of professional schools were also established. Schools for the training of teachers were divided into two groups: (1) those training teachers for elementary schools, and (2) higher normal schools, those training teachers for the middle schools. In this way the organization of schools was completed at the start of this century. Enrolment in the elementary schools reached more than 90%. For more than forty years after this the schools gradually expanded from the highest to the lowest classes of society, and they fulfilled their functions as schools for the entire nation.

Following conditions after the First World War, reforms were made in the educational systems of each nation. In Japan, after 1917, an educational conference was held in the cabinet where plans were made for educational reform. Accordingly, after 1919, the expansion of schools proceeded. The elementary schools of that time included six years of compulsory education and the enrolment reached 99%. From about this time those who advanced to higher studies increased in number. Also the number of those who entered into the various middle schools greatly increased, so that middle schools were expanded and supplementary education for business was built up. At this time, particularly, higher education was emphasized, and the former policy of not recognizing any university other than the Imperial Universities was changed and other public and private universities were recognized. Consequently, many private universities were established. Professional schools also increased. Thus, the problem of the expansion of the schools came to centre on middle and higher education. After the period of the growth of schools, Japan became one of the countries with universal education.

Not only school education but social education also was put in order in this period. This indicates that education expanded into spheres outside of the schools, too.

After 1932 a policy of strong control over education was adopted. The school system was not particularly altered but the practice of education gradually adopted a wartime character. After 1941 it became an emergency education system. The war ended in 1945, and in 1947 education was reformed. The so-called 6-3-3-4 system was established with nine years of elementary (6 years) and lower secondary (3 years) education being made compulsory. The practice of education in those schools underwent conspicuous change and constitutes present-day education in Japan.[1]

---

1 As to the detail, see *Education in Japan* compiled and published every two years by the Ministry of Education.

CHAPTER VI

The Elementary School and Its Development

The modern Japanese elementary school system was established after the Meiji Restoration. However, before this, there was a solid foundation in the elementary education bequeathed from the Edo period. For instance, there had already been calligraphy schools for the common people, the *terakoya, han* schools, and private seminars in various parts of the country. Each of these had different objectives and roles to play. These numerous schools were reorganized into the new educational programme of the Meiji period, especially in elementary school planning. Therefore, it was not the case that the elementary school systems of the Meiji period were established without some prior foundation for the common people. Without such a foundation, their rapid progress, seen from our present standpoint, would never have been possible.

The first attempt to create elementary schools in Japan was made immediately after the Meiji Restoration. The first school was that attached to the Numazu Military Academy, which was founded in 1868. Primarily, it was set up as a preparatory school for those entering the Military Academy. There elementary education was given to the children of the common people. The curriculum indicates its modern character, and it is evident that its model was the Western school system. The school in the city of Numazu was an exceptional case. However, in the city of Kyoto, a large-scale programme to establish elementary schools was drafted and enacted in 1869. The city was divided into several school districts, each having one elementary school. Above those districts, two larger divisions of Kamikyô (upper town) and Shimokyô (lower town) were created, in each of which the establishment of a middle school was planned. In this system, sixty-four elementary schools were opened in the same year for the sake of the people living in each district. The curriculum was based upon traditional courses handed down from the Edo period, but gradually new types of textbooks were adopted along with modern educational materials. In this programme, the running expenses of the elementary schools were the responsibility of the inhabitants of each district. That is to say, the schools received local financial support. Later, this became the pattern in various parts of the country and many elementary schools were established. It should be noted that these schools prepared the way for the formation of public elementary schools in later times.

The first nation-wide elementary school system was inaugurated in 1872 when the Government Order of Education was promulgated. But the project had already been planned shortly after the Meiji Restoration and proposals for the Order of Education had been prepared. In 1869 when the central government gave instructions to the newly created prefectural governments, provisions for the establishment of elementary school were included. The government intended to provide basic education for the inhabitants of each prefecture. They planned the schools to give courses in reading, writing and arithmetic necessary in the daily life of the people. They aimed also to give information about current affairs, and to furnish a moral education. Apart from schools for the common people, a special scheme of elementary schools was planned for the education of young leaders who were supposed to enter the middle schools and universities. It took form in the "Regulations for Universities, Middle and Elementary Schools". A curriculum was so arranged that, besides the study of general subjects, outlines corresponding to the five faculties of the university were taught. Further, in 1871, the Ministry of Education planned to establish elementary schools in Tokyo. They proclaimed in their educational policy that, for the sake of the development of the nation, it was essential to have the people send their children to the schools. Thus, the government began to clarify its policy to enforce the system of elementary schools. In 1872, the school system was promulgated after forming the plans for establishment of elementary schools through the five-year period after the Restoration. This was the origin of the system for the universalization of the elementary schools in Japan. In this system the elementary schools were the first stage of education, and it was stipulated that children from the age of six to fourteen should attend. At first, elementary school education was an eight-year system divided into lower elementary school, four years, and upper elementary school, four years. The plan was to have children enter the curriculum of the four-year lower elementary school, and when they completed the programme, advance to the four-year upper elementary school.

Various types of schools were conceived, having these standard periods. Girls' elementary schools, which primarily gave instruction in handicrafts, and village elementary schools for education appropriate to villagers and farmers, were established through donations. Elementary schools for the children of the poor, and the establishment of private schools in homes were also defined. It was clearly a policy that envisaged the preparation of many types of schools for many students.

The Ministry of Education established these elementary schools according to a system of school districts throughout the whole country and planned to set up 53,760 schools. Actually 25,000 schools were sufficient. One reason for the success of the policy in the five or six years after its enforcement was the fact that the country was minutely divided into districts with an elementary school designated for each area.

The types of subjects to be taught in the lower elementary schools included spelling, calligraphy, vocabulary, conversation, reading, ethics, letter writing, grammar, arithmetic, physical education, geography, and physics. In the upper elementary schools they offered such subjects as history, geometry, drawing, natural history, chemistry, and biology. This composition of the curriculum followed the order of the European elementary schools which they hoped to introduce similarly in Japan. However, this system of education differed considerably from both the content of popular education up till the Edo period which taught only reading, writing and the *soroban,* and the content of the warrior schools which taught Chinese by the method of *sodoku* (recitation). However, they could not carry this curriculum out immediately in the elementary schools. When the elementary schools were established, educators had to inform the public by means of the regulations mentioned above, that the curriculum had to be reformed in the manner of the European system.

The basic rules for the finance of the establishment of the elementary schools were also indicated in the Government Order of Education. Accordingly, the people in the school district, as a rule, bore the burden of the expense for the setting up and running of the schools. The parents of the children supplied an appropriate sum for the tuition. Besides that, the government subsidized the expense of education in each district. Thus, they tried to provide for the cost of the elementary schools with three methods, but there were many difficulties. The subsidy from the national treasury was extremely small, and the greater part of the cost fell to the residents of each area. Because of this, there was a tendency to dislike the establishment and administration of the schools. With the adoption of whichever method was suitable to the region, the establishment and administration of the schools gradually progressed. The people in each school district began to recognize the importance of education, and an attitude of co-operation began to appear.

Hence, first steps were taken to make the elementary schools universal according to the Government Order of Education of 1872. We will determine below from a number of points how the elementary schools, from that time to the present, became universal and became schools belonging to the people.

We must first inquire into the arrangements for the development of the elementary schools. As we have already made clear, the elementary schools were divided into lower and upper, each division requiring four years, in the 1872 school system. Because this was only a plan on paper, it became necessary to reexamine the whole scheme of elementary schools on the basis of experience after the establishment of the Government Order.

The whole school system was reformed by the Education Law of 1880. In 1881, the Instruction for Elementary School Education was promulgated and the elementary school course was divided into three time periods: primary level, three years; middle, three years; and higher level, two years. This was designed to give a complete elementary education in eight years. Since attendance in the four-year lower elementary school became a problem, a three-year first stage was provided in order, first of all, to encourage greater attendance. The plan was intended to stimulate students to enter the three-year middle course and to bring about the universalization of elementary school education by facing the actual problems of the time. When the Elementary School Order was again issued in 1886 following observation of the progress of attendance in the elementary schools, the government organized the system into four-year ordinary elementary school, and four-year upper elementary school. For the children who could not attend the ordinary elementary school, a simplified three-year half-day course was provided. Since at that time half the number of children eligible under the school law could not attend owing to the lack of school facilities, it was very difficult to expand elementary school education to agricultural and fishing villages with just the four-year course of ordinary elementary education. In 1890, this problem was no longer so pressing, and the ordinary elementary school was changed to three or four years while the simplified course of half-day schools was abolished. In this way the system of elementary education was gradually elevated.

In 1900, the whole system was again completely reformed. Every aspect of elementary education was adjusted. The years of attendance in the ordinary primary school increased to four, and the three-year course was abolished. Later in 1907, when the period of compulsory education was lengthened by two years, the ordinary elementary school became six years. In this system, upper primary school was either two or three years. The elementary school system of 6–2 became the basic system of elementary education in Japan for the next forty years. The students who received six years of elementary education advanced to middle schools. Hence, elementary schools took shape in which six years' attendance constituted a complete course. Students who did not progress to the middle school advanced to the upper elementary school and there received general education.

As indicated above, the elementary schools were first planned as eight-year schools in two stages of four years each, then in stages of 3-3-2, and again in a 4-4 system with a three-year simplified course. The simplified course was then abolished and ordinary elementary school consisted of 3 or 4 years. Following this, the 4-4 system was again changed to a 6-2 system. The following diagram will indicate how the 6-2 system was arrived at through adapting a policy of gradually lengthening the period of compulsory school attendance:

	Elementary School		Middle School	
1872		4	4	8
1881	3	3	2	8
1886		6	4	10
	3	(Simplified Course)		
1890		4	4	8
	3	(Simplified Course)		
1902		4	4	8
1907		6	2	8
1947		6	3	9

Following the 1947 reforms, the elementary schools came to consist of a six-year course and the two-year upper elementary school was transformed into the three-year middle school, so that all the students, who were obliged to choose one of the two types of school systems after the six years of elementary school, are now attending a unitary system of compulsory middle school. It was a remarkable change in the upper section of elementary school education.

How did the enrolment of students progress in the course of the development of the elementary school system? The Government Order of Education was promulgated in 1872, but in the next year, the enrolment percentage in elementary schools was 28.13; 39.9 per cent of boys and hardly 15.14 per cent of girls were enrolled. At this time there were 12,597 elementary schools, and the total number of students was 1,326,190. In 1875, the number of schools increased to 24,303 and the number of students reached 1,926,126. These schools were considered indispensable for Japan. The following chart shows clearly the increase in the number of students after this year.

YEAR	TOTAL PERCENTAGE	BOYS	GIRLS
1875	35.19	50.49	18.58
1880	41.06	58.72	21.91
1885	49.62	65.80	32.07
1890	48.93	65.14	31.13
1895	61.24	76.65	43.87
1900	81.48	90.55	71.73
1905	95.62	97.72	93.34
1910	98.14	98.83	97.38
1915	98.47	98.93	97.96
1920	99.03	99.20	98.84
1925	99.43	99.47	99.38
1930	99.51	99.52	99.50
1935	99.59	99.59	99.59
1940	99.64	99.64	99.65
1945	99.79	99.78	99.81
1950	99.63	99.75	99.65

1955	99.77	99.75	99.78
1960	99.82	99.79	99.83

As is indicated in this chart, the number of students enrolled in school jumped remarkably about 1895. In 1902, it reached more than 90%, by 1909, 98%, and after 1925, it was more than 99% of both boys and girls. It has remained so to the present time. In the following chart we give the years 1890 to 1910, during which period the number of children attending school greatly increased.

YEAR	TOTAL PERCENTAGE
1890	48.93
1895	61.24
1896	64.22
1897	66.65
1898	68.91
1899	72.75
1900	81.48
1901	88.05
1902	91.57
1903	93.23
1904	94.43
1905	95.62
1906	96.51
1907	97.38
1908	97.83
1909	98.10
1910	98.14

To achieve a higher standard of living through industrialization, primary education was deemed essential. Thus, great efforts were made to reduce the number of those not attending school. The Ministry of Education at that time had a policy to universalize schools and to raise the standard of living. Also, the modernization of industry progressed during this period. The new industries, and particularly manufacturing, would not be possible with widespread illiteracy.

From about the year 1893, the standard of living of the Japanese people became higher through the development of industries. Consequently, the movement to attend school among the common people increased. On the strength of this increase the elementary school law was revised in 1900, and the obligation to attend school was defined in more detail. Legal guardians and those who employed children had to carry out their obligation to permit them to attend school. Together with this clarification of policy, it was also made clear who could postpone his schooling or be exempted from attendance.

As a result of the prescripts of this elementary school law, the number of students in the schools increased greatly after 1900. In 1902, the percentages of the attendance of both boys and girls became more than 90% in average. The number in attendance, 41% in 1880, increased 50% in twenty years. In 1909, it became 98%. The basic national strength of Japan at that time is reflected in this increase. After 1920, it reached more than 99% which supported the industrial development of Japan after the First World War and the raising of the standard of living of the people.

After 1908, the period of compulsory elementary education was extended from four to six years, but the percentage of students attending did not decrease as a result of this. The six-year period was thought appropriate, and the number attending increased. This period was thought appropriate because the number of students continuing on for an additional two years after the ordinary elementary school had increased even without its being compulsory.

In the school system of 1872, the Ministry of Education began an eight-year elementary school system, and declared that all children could attend. However, they could not achieve that goal immediately. It required some thirty years to bring the number of students attending school to 90%, but it would require another twenty years to have 99% of all the children subject to the school law attend school. In 1873, the number of students attending was approximately 27% of those eligible. Only 15% of eligible girls were enrolled. After about fifty years the total reached 99% of those eligible when the ideal of "no family without primary education" was finally realized. In the first year of Meiji (1868), more than 70% of the children did not attend school, and illiteracy, nation-wide, was more than 80%. In order to progress from this condition to that of almost no illiteracy required repeated efforts over half a century to reform and administer the elementary school system in order to increase the attendance.

We must now investigate what kind of courses were employed. In these elementary schools, from the year 1872, the Ministry of Education devised a modern school curriculum. The subjects offered in the schools had to be modern according to the dictates of official policy. However, the elementary schools of this time employed the three basic subjects of reading, writing and *soroban* (arithmetic with abacus) which had been given in the popular *terakoya* of the Edo period. These three subjects were considered necessary in the elementary schools, but there were efforts to modernize their contents. Calligraphy had been regarded as the essence of learning in the popular schools of Edo and took up most of the learning time. In the new system this was changed. The authorities increased reading materials, using text books which could enable students to understand the new culture and way of life. Up to that time the *soroban* or abacus had been the basis of education in arithmetic. The method of calculation based on figures was employed in teaching the fundamentals of modern mathematics. Consequently, the elementary school course did not go beyond the fortress of the 3 R's.

However, in the arithmetic of the higher elementary schools of the advanced countries of the West, education in the 3 R's had already been reformed into a modern course. Because the Japanese educators planned an elementary school course based on that of Europe, they stipulated in the 1872 school plan that the elementary school curriculum should contain 14 subjects: spelling, calligraphy, vocabulary, conversation, reading, ethics, letter writing, grammar, arithmetic, hygiene, geography, science, physical education and music. In the upper elementary school, further, outlines of history, geometry (drafting), natural history, chemistry and physiology were stipulated. So long as they offered this large number of subjects, they could not carry out this programme immediately in the elementary schools of that time. Therefore, the educators organized the curriculum on the basis of the actual elementary school education of that time. Using this as the standard, they reformed education in reading, writing and abacus. For this purpose, they invited M. M. Scott[1] to the normal school as an advisor and began to modernize the school curriculum. Accordingly, they formulated a curriculum including subjects, such as reading, arithmetic, writing, stenography, composition, discussion, recitation and physical education. Among the subjects of reading and discussion, studies in geography, history, natural history, physics, chemistry and ethics were included.

When the elementary school system of 1881 was reformed, the curriculum was also renovated. In the beginning of the three-year elementary curriculum, ethics, reading, writing, arithmetic and physical education were included. The three-year middle curriculum included ethics, reading, writing, arithmetic, geography, Japanese history, drawing, natural history, physics, needlework and physical education. In the final two-year higher course, ethics, reading, writing, arithmetic, geography, drawing, natural history, chemistry, biology, geometry, economics, needlework, home economics and physical education were taught. The content was defined and time allotted to each of these subjects. In this way educators established a basic modern course for the first time. It was not immediately enforced in the elementary schools of that time, but the curriculum was gradually arranged and adjusted based on this ideal.

About this time, students attended only the first three years of the elementary school course. In this basic curriculum, ethics and physical education were added to reading, writing and arithmetic. While the

---

1 Marion M. Scott (1843-1922), an American educator who taught at *Daigaku Nankô* (the present University of Tokyo) in 1871, then at the Tokyo Normal School after 1872, made a remarkable contribution in the development of normal schools in Japan.

curriculum was based on the 3 R's, it was planned to have education develop by adding new subjects in the middle and higher levels.

On the occasion of the reform of the educational system in 1886, the formulation of the curriculum was changed. During the four-year period of the ordinary elementary school, the subjects of ethics, reading, writing, arithmetic, music and physical education were included. In the upper elementary school, the subjects of ethics, reading, composition, writing, arithmetic, geography, history, science, drawing, music, physical education and needlework were taught. From this period, the curriculum of the elementary school was officially defined and put into effect in each school.

When the period of compulsory education was extended in 1907, the ordinary elementary school course became six years in length. Because of this, the curriculum had to be renovated again. At this time, the curriculum was composed of ethics, Japanese, arithmetic, Japanese history, geography, science, drawing, music, physical education, needlework, and handicrafts.

In the lower grades the five subjects of ethics, Japanese, arithmetic, music and physical education were offered, while in the middle grades drawing and needlework were added. Further, in the upper grades, Japanese history and science were introduced. This organization of the curriculum was again changed in 1940. And after 1947, ethics, geography and history were abolished, and a new social studies' curriculum was created. This became the present educational setup of Japan.

At present, the elementary school education curriculum is divided into four general parts. These are curriculum, special education activities, school affairs and ethics. All educational activities are arranged in these four areas. The curriculum consists of Japanese, arithmetic, social studies, science, drawing, crafts, music, domestic science, physical education. With respect to these subjects, each school determines its schedule for the week based on the number of hours in the week in the curriculum, and with ethics established separately as shown in the following chart:

Subjects	Year–I	II	III	IV	V	VI
Japanese	7	9	8	8	7	7
Social Studies	2	2	3	4	4	4
Arithmetic	3	4	5	6	6	6
Science	2	2	3	3	4	4
Music	3	2	2	2	2	2
Drawing–Crafts	3	2	2	2	2	2
Domestic Science	–	–	–	–	2	2
Physical Education	3	3	3	3	3	3
Ethics	1	1	1	1	1	1
Total	24	25	27	29	31	31

Special educational activities includes pupils' general assembly, class organizations and club activity. School activities refer to ceremonies, gym meets, literary exercises and school excursions.

Teaching these subjects required teaching materials and equipment. Most important were textbooks. In the Edo period *terakoya,* the teachers wrote the texts as models in calligraphy. These were given to the students who used them as textbooks to be read. Most of these textbooks were not published. Since they gave instruction in computation using the abacus, the students did not particularly make use of study textbooks for arithmetic. Hence, textbooks used before the Meiji period were very limited in number. In the Meiji period, the Ministry of Education adopted the policy of spreading education appropriate to the age through the use of textbooks in the elementary schools. In order to materialize this policy, the Ministry set up an editorial organization and published various new textbooks as samples. Following these examples, several commercial publishers started compiling textbooks which were published and used in the elementary schools. At that time, since textbooks were hitherto nonexistent in the fields of geography, foreign history, natural history, physics and chemistry, European texts were imported and translated. Because computation with figures in arithmetic was new, the Ministry published translations of texts used in elementary schools of the West. As the idea at the time was to accept Western texts as quickly as possible for the sake of cultural enlightenment, Japanese readers were also translated textbooks. The American *Wilson Reader* was translated and published by the Ministry of Education as an elementary reader. The text was spread throughout the country. Wall maps were also compiled by the Ministry. The maps which hung in the classroom and used in teaching, were taken to be signs of cultural enlightenment by the Japanese people of that period.

From about 1880 on, the use of translated textbooks declined. Particularly, the movement to formulate and produce textbooks based on Japanese national culture and thought became strong. Ethics was taught in textbooks of Oriental morals based on Confucianism. Foreign history was not offered in the elementary schools, but textbooks dealing with Japanese history were compiled and used.

Under such circumstances, the use of textbooks which were considered not pertinent for elementary schools was prohibited. Among them were books designed to inculcate the ideas of civil rights and democracy. Thus, the adoption of textbooks, which had hitherto been completely free, now required a report to the Ministry. The authorities also adopted a textbook policy which prohibited the use of unauthorized texts. Further, the Ministry of Education indicated a strong interest in the content of textbooks. After the reform of the system in 1886, they adopted a method of inspecting texts. At this time, the Ministry compiled and published texts which were to serve as standards for privately published books. Among these were many with new arrangements hitherto unseen in textbooks, and they had great influence on the private compiling of elementary school texts.

However, after 1903, a new policy was adopted in which elementary school textbooks were written by the Ministry of Education and all elementary schools used the same texts. From this time till the 1947 reform, which called for its abolishment, this state textbook system was enforced. For a period of forty years, state textbooks were employed in every school. After the establishment of state texts in all subjects, no other textbooks were used, and privately published textbooks were abolished completely.

After the 1947 reform, the Ministry of Education stopped writing textbooks and initiated a policy of investigating and adopting texts privately compiled. Because privately compiled texts had as their standard the *Gakushû Shidô Yôryô* (Essentials of Educational Leadership), they were not entirely freely authored. A limit was imposed on the number of pages, but there was more freedom, and a variety of texts was compiled. Textbooks of the elementary schools in Japan had formerly been purchased by the guardians or parents. Most recently, the free textbook system has been established, and books which pass inspection are purchased at national expense and given to the students. Consequently, the burden on the parents of buying texts has disappeared.

After the beginning of Meiji, the elementary schools imported new educational methods and renovated the earlier methods of the *terakoya*. The most striking thing was that the individual tutelage method of the *terakoya* was changed, and new methods of group teaching were formulated for all grades. These new methods were tried out in the elementary schools attached to the Tokyo Normal School. They placed thirty or forty students into one class and gave instruction to all of the students together at one time. This method of simultaneous teaching was attempted also by American instructors who taught teachers gathered from all over the country. Each provincial normal school put the method into practice. Consequently, together with the new textbooks, the new methods of teaching also spread.

After 1880, Professor Hideo Takamine, who had studied the Pestalozzi method at the Oswego Normal School in America, introduced it to Japan. It had as its basis, teaching through direct observation, and employed the method of dialogue in order to develop the minds of the growing students. This method moved in the direction of reforming the procedure of merely lecturing and reading the materials of the basic textbooks. However, the method in which the teacher arranged and used materials to teach the students could not be changed immediately by this movement.

After 1887, the theory of teaching of the Herbartian school[1] was
introduced from Germany, and the concept of teaching in stages became
influential in the educational world. It adopted a method of teaching
arranged in five stages and was intended to instill ideas into students. The
method spread to schools throughout the nation. With this method, the
teacher first prepared the materials and instilled them into the students,
and then had the students arrange his information into organized knowledge, so that they could put their knowledge to practical use. This
method fixed the direction of teaching in the elementary schools.

There were those who opposed this method of instilling knowledge
in students and advocated the spontaneity of their will to study. After
1915 especially, a new movement in education, the so-called "new education" arose in every country throughout the world. There were
teachers in Japanese schools who were attracted to the new method.
They advocated reform in educational methods. However, before this
new method penetrated the teaching of the elementary schools, conditions after 1930 required that teachers drill students and adapt education
to respond to national crisis. During the Second World War, the government controlled education, bringing it into line with its war policy, and
methods for encouraging the students' voluntary efforts to study disappeared. Students were trained as faithful subjects to serve the country.

After 1945, education was reformed from its very foundations, and
democratic methods of education, which encouraged independent action
on the part of the students, were adopted in elementary schools under
the slogan "new education". This type of education has been most influential since the 1947 reform of the education system.

The most recent count of elementary schools totals about 26,600, and
the students attending about 11,500,000. They have spread to all agricultural, fishing and other villages throughout the country, and they
are provided for and administered so that all children of the age for

---

1 Johann Friedrich Herbart (1776-1841), student of Pestalozzi, developed a pedagogical
method on the basis of association psychology dividing the education process into five
stages: preparation, presentation, association, generalization and application.

compulsory education can attend. The equipment of the various metropolitan elementary schools has recently been improved. Elementary schools in remote areas particularly have been expanded, and policies for raising the standard of education of those areas have been adopted. In order to achieve this, subsidies are received from the national government.

Further, scientific education has been promoted in elementary schools. For this purpose, appropriate sums have been given, and gradually the equipment has become sufficient. Also supplementary funds have been given for school libraries. Radio and television have gradually spread to the elementary schools and are useful in teaching. In Japanese elementary schools, it was planned that each class should have about fifty students, but since in some schools there were more than fifty per class, an effort has been made to reduce the number to below fifty. In the future it is hoped that this will be decreased further to below forty pupils.

For pre-school education, kindergartens were set up after 1875. They have spread remarkably in recent times, their number now being about 7,500. The number of pupils is about 857,000. Kindergarten education is not compulsory, but a policy has been adopted to promote it in order to spread pre-school education. Numerous kindergartens are provided in the cities. In the agricultural villages, many nursery schools are provided by social welfare. All these efforts together are producing considerable improvement in child education at the pre-school level.

CHAPTER VII

The Development of Middle School Education

The First Stage in the Planning of Middle Schools

Many schools had already been set up in the Edo period, but no schools providing secondary education had yet been established. After the Meiji Restoration, the new government developed plans for schools. They called the educational institutions which came between the elementary and higher schools "middle schools".

The city of Kyoto formulated the earliest policy for providing middle school or secondary education. The educational authorities there in 1868 planned to set up schools according to a system of school districts. At that time, they considered the schools provided for the graduates of the elementary schools as middle schools. According to its policy, Kyoto set up two middle schools. It was so arranged that from among the graduates of these schools would come the students who would proceed to the university which the government provided.

In 1870, the government published its plans concerning the organization of schools in order to construct a university system. At that time, referring to the Kyoto plans, it considered the middle schools as those providing the fundamental education required for entrance to the university. It allowed sixteen-year-old students who had graduated from elementary school to enter middle school to pursue specialized studies. The specialized subjects were divided into five areas as in the university, *i.e.,* teaching, law, letters, science, and medicine. It was stipulated that only the most excellent individuals from among the students who graduated from middle school could enter the university at the age of twenty-two.

This system was not put into effect immediately throughout the nation, but in 1870 two years after middle schools were begun in Kyoto, they were also established in Tokyo. There were cases in the regions of the feudal clans in which the old clan schools of the Edo period were reformed and administered with the title middle school. Thus, with the government's proclamation of the school system's being composed of elementary school, middle school and university, the role of the middle school was made clear as an institution for secondary education.

However, it was not until 1872 that schools for secondary education were stipulated in detail by law in the Government Order of Education *(Gakusei)*. In the Order, which determined the entire school system of Japan, the middle schools were to teach a general curriculum to students who had passed through the elementary schools. These middle schools were divided into upper and lower divisions. Besides these, various schools, such as technical, commercial, agricultural and foreign language schools were listed in the Order. According to this Order, there were (1) middle schools for giving ordinary secondary education, (2) vocational schools for technical, commercial, agricultural and foreign language education, and (3) evening schools for working people. This Order provided detailed regulations concerning middle schools, but for the other schools, merely their classification and character were indicated. Middle schools were set up, one school to one middle school district. There were plans to set up 256 schools throughout the country. Children from fourteen to sixteen years of age were to attend the lower division of the middle school. Students from seventeen to nineteen entered the upper division.

The lower and upper middle schools were three years each, six years in total. The provisions of the school system stipulated the content of the general curriculum given in these schools. The promulgation of the *Chûgaku Kyôsoku Ryaku* defined the curriculum in more detail. Thus, the middle schools provided the substance of secondary education, and they

were set up first of all. The vocational schools were to be established
later, but a concrete plan was not made public.

Further, since the curriculum and teaching materials of the middle
schools were insufficient, it was decided to provide middle schools taught
by foreign teachers and using foreign textbooks. In order to be able to
comprehend the courses given by foreign teachers in a foreign language,
the students had to take a one year preparatory course in the language
before entering middle school. However, because these middle schools
were designed to give higher education, they were soon reformed into
institutions of higher education. Thus, among the middle schools, various forms of education were carried out in schools which had not yet
been formally arranged as institutions of secondary education. Consequently, schools which provided education above the primary level were
all considered middle schools.

Since these middle schools preceded the establishment of the universities, they can be viewed as the institutions with which secondary education began. According to the report of the Ministry of Education of 1875,
there were 116 such middle schools in the country. Eleven were public
schools, while 105 were privately established. There were 5,620 students,
and among them there were 183 girls. Eighty per cent of the private
schools were set up in Tokyo. Among these there were private schools
for teaching only one or two subjects. These were also called middle
schools, but they differed from the middle schools set up in the school
districts by the Government Order of Education of 1872.

The education law of 1881 redefined in greater detail the system of
middle schools. The education law stated that the middle schools were
to give a higher general education. They were to be considered as schools
for providing education for those who would either take jobs above the
middle grade or proceed to a higher school.

Divided into a junior course of four years and a senior course of two
years, the middle school provided six years of secondary education.
Since elementary schools had been established throughout the country,
those who completed the six-year primary education course, that is,
those who finished the intermediate course of the elementary school,

were qualified to proceed to the middle school. Thus, the relation between the elementary and middle schools became clearer. It was the beginning of the system in which middle school education followed upon the six-year primary education.

In 1881, the education law also provided for vocational education in which agricultural, commercial and technical schools were classified as middle schools. In 1883, new rules were laid down for the agricultural schools, and for the business schools in 1884. Detailed regulations were specified.

At this time vocational schools were divided into two types. The first type consisted of a two-year course for students who completed the six-year elementary school course. The second type provided a three-year education for those who had completed the four-year middle school curriculum. The first type was designed for industrial education. The second type gave training to those who would be managers in industry. This marked the beginning of the educational policy of the government pertaining to vocational schools. In 1884 there were twenty-six industrial schools and 990 students. The spread of vocational schools is related to the development of industry. But as the Japanese industry of that period was still at the primitive level, the way for the development of secondary vocational schools had not as yet been paved. Since industry was, as yet, not much advanced, the technical schools could not be adopted as special or separate part of the system. The middle schools which related to these industries were set up for the first time when Japanese industry made conspicuous progress in the period after 1895.

The Organization of Middle Schools

Thus, nature of the middle schools was not yet clarified, and the nature of the vocational schools was still in the first stage of experimentation. However, the renovation of the entire school system in 1886 with the promulgation of the Middle School Order resulted in the reorganization of the institutions of secondary education into a completely different form. Schools were divided into three stages: elementary, middle and university.

The middle schools received graduates of the elementary schools while the graduates of the middle schools similarly could advance to the universities. The middle schools, which were institutions of secondary education, were divided into ordinary middle school and higher middle school. In each prefecture, as a rule, one ordinary middle school was administered at public expense. The Ministry Education of administered the higher middle schools, and there were five such schools in the country. The Ministry paid for these schools from funds derived from the regional taxes of the prefectures in each district and from the national treasury. Under this new system, the institutions of secondary education were in two stages, about fifty ordinary middle schools throughout the country and five higher middle schools for the graduates in each district. After graduating from higher middle school, students could enter the Imperial Universities. The higher middle schools later became the higher schools and preparatory schools for the university. They formed one part of the higher educational structure.

As a result of the reorganization of the system, the middle school course became five years. In order to matriculate, students had to be a full twelve years of age or older. Consequently, those students who completed the two years of upper elementary school and the six years of elementary education could enter middle school. This clarified the relation between the length of time of the later middle school and elementary education by requiring six years of elementary school and five years of middle school comprising a course of eleven years. The middle school provided a higher general education, including courses in ethics, language, and Chinese classics, a first and second foreign languages, agriculture, geography, history, mathematics, natural science, physics, chemistry, calligraphy, art, poetry, and physical education. The graduates of this higher middle school could advance to a higher level school or take positions in business. To achieve either goal, a student of middle school could elect to take up special courses in agriculture, technology or business. It was the policy to provide vocational education according to the conditions in the area. However, they were different in nature from the vocational schools.

Following such a policy, the Ministry of Education set up ordinary middle schools. After that, the number of schools recognized as ordinary middle schools decreased, as did the number of students. It was owing to the fact that the middle schools, which up to that time had not sufficiently fulfilled their functions as institutions of secondary education, was more clearly defined institutionally. Their curricula and methods of teaching were also reformed, and much higher level of middle schools were created. Since only one middle school, publicly established according to this policy in each prefecture, was recognized, it was usually set up in the central city of each prefecture, where students came from all over the prefecture to enter the school. As a result, people thought of the schools as similar to the clan schools of the Edo period. Because elementary schools were not yet universalized at that time, those attending the elementary schools were less than half the number eligible under the school law. Consequently, most of the students who progressed to middle school were children of the families who had been the warriors of the old clans. According to the education statistics for 1890, there were fifty-five ordinary middle schools with 11,620 students. Only selected boys could enter the middle schools. The children of the general citizens were not permitted to enter these schools. Due to this situation, the middle schools drew their students from families of the middle and upper classes. The people generally recognized these schools as those to which students with ability progressed and as institutions which provided the highest level of education among the secondary schools. A great many of their graduates went on for higher education. As a result, the status of the middle school improved.

By no means did all the graduates of the middle schools, however, go on for higher education. Eighty per cent took up an occupation. Therefore, it was planned that, besides the general education of the middle schools, students could select subjects useful for their occupations. This policy was not successful because technical schools on the secondary level were separately provided as middle schools designed to give education needed in industry. Also, the industrial world employed graduates of middle school in office and managerial positions. Because of this, the idea spread widely through the populace that boys with ability proceeded to middle schools. Later, as a result of this situation, the middle school system was studied several times and reformed, but the character of the middle schools as schools of the highest standard in the direct line of secondary education remained unchanged. After the turn of the century the pupils of elementary schools gradually increased, and the number desiring to enter the middle schools conspicuously augmented. The expansion of the schools may be indicated in the following chart of the number of schools and students:

Year	Schools	Students
1890	55	11,620
1895	96	30,871
1900	218	78,315
1905	271	104,968
1910	311	122,345
1915	321	141,954
1920	368	177,201
1925	368	177,201
1930	557	345,691
1935	557	340,657
1940	600	432,288
1945	776	639,756

The Institutionalization of Girls' High Schools

The middle schools gave a secondary level general education to boys. For girls, the girls' high schools were set up separately from the middle schools. Like the boys' middle schools, they developed as schools which gave a general education. Coeducation was not practised in the middle schools, as it had been traditionally thought that the education of boys was of a different nature from that of girls. As a result of this way of thinking, the girls' high schools developed over a long period of time a special character as schools for providing education which differed from that of the middle schools.

In 1871 the Ministry of Education proclaimed the establishment of a government-sponsored girls' school in Tokyo. This was the beginning of providing secondary education for girls. Later, a number of girls' secondary schools similar to the school set up by the government were founded. Some of these schools had the name Girls' Middle School. In 1882, after the establishment of a girls' high school within the Tokyo Women's Normal School, the names of the girls' middle schools were made uniform under the name girls' high school.

Girls who completed the six-year course in the elementary schools entered these schools where they then received a five-year education. At that time the curricula in the boys' and girls' schools were clearly differentiated. The curricula of the girls' high schools included ethics for women, etiquette, home economics, the care of children, sewing and handicrafts, in addition to the general curriculum. Gradually the number of schools for giving higher education to girls, and the number of their students increased.

However, at first, these schools had no independent status within the complete school system. For the first time in 1893, stipulations governing the girls' high schools were established and the schools were institutionalized. On that occasion the people regarded the girls' schools as being on a slightly lower level than that of the boys. They required for entrance eligibility only that one graduate from a four-year elementary school course. The period for completion of the course was six years. Thus, in comparison with the boys' middle schools, the girls entered a year earlier and graduated a year earlier.

Later, in 1899, a law on girls' high schools was promulgated, and the organization further changed. At that time, also, the requirement of completion of six years of elementary school was made the same as in

the case of the boys' schools. The period of study, four years being regarded as standard, could be lengthened or shortened by one year. Consequently, the length of study was revised to cover three to five years.
According to the circumstances, in comparison with the middle schools,
a two-year difference was possible. Further, because they added domestic
science and sewing to the girls' curriculum, the content of the general
curriculum was simpler than that of the middle schools. They especially
simplified the physical sciences and mathematics, and in addition decided
that foreign languages could be omitted. In 1910, practical courses, primarily home economics, were instituted. In these practical courses, students who graduated from the upper elementary schools were accepted,
and according to the circumstances, the length of the course was shortened one or two years.

Since generally it was believed at that time that a girl's education was
sufficiently provided for by the girls' high schools, no provision was
made for their entrance into the university. Therefore, the Ministry of
Education set up a system to prepare the girls for being housewives at
the level of secondary education. As a result, it established various forms
of girls' middle schools.

In 1895 there were fifteen girls' high schools and 2,897 students. They
later made outstanding progress, becoming institutions of secondary
education with more students than the boys' middle schools. The following chart indicates the number of schools and students:

Year	Schools	Students
1895	15	2,897
1900	52	11,984
1905	100	31,918
1910	193	56,239
1915	366	95,949
1920	514	151,288
1925	805	301,447
1930	975	368,999
1935	974	412,126

| 1940 | 1066 | 555,589 |
| 1945 | 1272 | 875,814 |

The Institutionalization of Vocational Schools

While the term vocational schools was employed from early times, their institutionalization as places for secondary education had been planned separately from that of middle school and no independent system of secondary schools for vocational education was created for a considerable length of time. From about 1893, following an increase in production, a policy of providing schools for persons engaged in industry was introduced. Manufacturing became the centre of the new industrial production and it was required that these new schools had to produce factory workers and did so by providing industrial education on the secondary level for the important industries. To achieve their purpose, they planned to establish apprentice schools.

Graduates of elementary schools could enrol in these new schools and pursue a course of study varying from six months to four years. Besides the general curriculum which included ethics, arithmetic, geometry, physics, chemistry and drawing, students trained for jobs in factories following a practical curriculum. Further, the Ministry set up simple agricultural schools for those whose occupations were on farms. During the slack agricultural season, the village youth would commute to these schools and receive instruction to aid in promoting agricultural production. Graduates of the elementary schools from the ages of fourteen and above could enrol in these schools. Separate from such schools, the government planned and regulated the establishment of supplementary vocational schools. There the graduates of elementary school who were engaging in actual work were given necessary instruction in techniques of industry.

The curriculum included ethics, reading, writing, calligraphy and arithmetic, as well as simplified agriculture, business and industrial subjects. The period of training was three years and the schools were opened Sundays and evenings in order to supplement the education of the working people. The government subsidized the cost of vocational education from the national treasury. As a result, Japanese industry made remarkable progress from the end of the nineteenth century into the twentieth. Vocational education as a whole advanced through the new system. Consequently, the vocational schools took their place in the system of secondary education. The organization of these schools differed from the middle schools and girls' high schools because any graduate of the elementary schools could enrol.

In 1899 the Vocational School Order was promulgated completing the institutionalization of the schools. At this time, there were five types of vocational schools: namely, technical, agricultural, commercial, mercantile marine, and supplementary vocational schools. The government stipulated that eight years of elementary school education were to be completed for entrance. These schools gave an additional four years of education. In this way the technical schools became secondary schools. After the end of the First World War, the government expanded the system of technical schools as students entering secondary schools increased in number. The following chart indicates this development in the number of schools and students:

Year	Schools	Students
1890	23	2,435
1895	45	5,015
1900	116	15,233
1905	158	29,959
1910	204	40,619
1915	206	50,743
1920	279	84,440
1925	528	171,490
1930	786	252,965
1935	961	333,939

1940	1,207	535,826
1945	1,743	845,497

Most of the education of the supplementary vocational schools which formed one part of the vocational school system took place in the evenings in the elementary school buildings. The number of students increased, but the results of these schools do not appear to have been outstanding.

In 1926, the Ministry of Education and the Bureau of the Army cooperated in setting up training institutes for young men of the same age level. A military training policy was adopted and young men from the ages of sixteen to twenty, entering the institutes, received a part-time education in the evenings for four years. Besides the general and vocational subjects, they received military drill. The youths who completed the course could enter the army. The year the programme began, the government announced that there were 15,588 institutes and 891,555 students. Thus, there were two types of educational institutions available to most working youths. In 1935 the government combined the supplementary vocational schools and the training institutes to form youth schools. They designed these schools for students who graduated from the upper elementary school course. For boys the length of the regular course was five years and for girls it was three years.

In 1939 the regular course of the part-time evening youth schools became obligatory. This change conformed to the policy of strengthening military training. Together with the provision of publicly sponsored youth schools to provide this compulsory education in each town and village, the government authorized private youth schools in factories and places of employment for youths working there. Thus, the youth schools were responsible for the education of those who graduated from the elementary schools but who did not enrol in the secondary schools. Since most of the students who graduated from the six-year elementary school received five years of additional education by graduating from the two-year upper elementary school and entering the youth school, they received a total of thirteen years of education including elementary

$$6 + 2 + 3 + 2 = 13$$

school. The following chart indicates the number of educational institutions including the supplementary vocational schools and the youth schools and the number of registered students:

Year	Schools	Students
1900	151	8,880
1905	2,746	121,502
1910	6,111	262,978
1915	8,908	498,178
1920	14,232	996,020
1925	15,316	1,051,437
1930	15,248	1,277,338
1935	16,705	1,902,157
1940	20,492	2,619,684
1945	15,144	2,606,990

The Parallel System of Secondary Education

As we have indicated above, the system of secondary education in Japan became increasingly complicated during the eighty-year period after the beginning of Meiji. The government considered the schools where the graduates of the six-year elementary school course later enrolled entirely as institutions for giving a secondary education. The schools to which most of the students advanced were the two-year upper elementary school which was part of the elementary school system and the regular five-year youth school which followed the two-year upper elementary school. This system was a combination of a two-year system of daily education and a five-year part-time system. About eighty per cent of the elementary school graduates advanced through this system. However, they actually received a secondary education. Systematically speaking, the Ministry treated such schools as extended elementary schools, and did not recognize them as secondary schools. Thus, a wall separated the system of the upper elementary school-youth school and that of the middle schools. In such youth schools more than two million students received an education until the age of nineteen.

About twenty per cent of elementary school graduates enrolled in the secondary schools. These were selected students. Of the three types of the secondary schools, namely, middle schools, girls' high schools, and vocational schools, the middle schools and the girls' high schools had the task of teaching the general curriculum on the secondary level. However, the middle schools were for boys and the history of their establishment is the oldest of the three. And the authorities treated them as representative of secondary education and they became the main line among the secondary schools. Consequently, when the other types of secondary schools were established, superior students entered the middle schools. And those who went on for advanced education were chosen from the middle school graduates. Thus, the middle schools had the highest status among the three types of secondary schools. The girls' high schools gave a general education to girls on the same level as the middle schools and were similarly designed to give a higher education. Actually, however, as is mentioned above, they were thought to be on a lower level. The organization of the school year differed and the curriculum was adapted to the aims of feminine education. Consequently, the girls' high schools developed a different character from that of the boys. The graduates of the girls' high schools could enrol in special schools, but since there were no advanced girls' schools, the government did not officially recognize their entering the Imperial university or other public or private universities. It was not only that the secondary schools were not coeducational, but the girls' high schools were administered differently from the boys' schools.

The vocational schools belonged to a separate school system from the middle schools. The educational authorities regarded the vocational schools as being on a lower level than that of the middle schools and girls' high schools which provided a general education. It came from the fact that working in industry was generally regarded as a lower class job and the government officials, the office workers and the managerial

group were considered as having a higher status. Further, the graduates
of the vocational schools immediately took jobs and they usually did not
go on for advanced education. As a result, they were treated accordingly

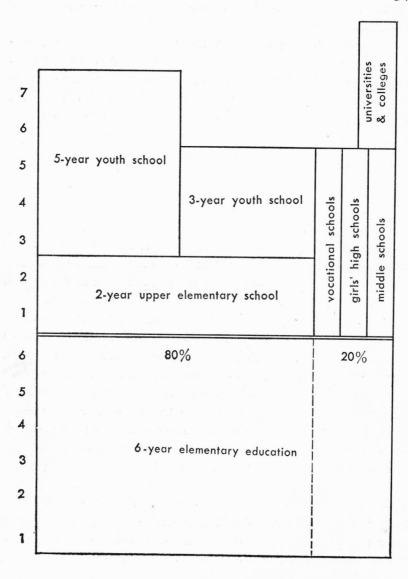

in the institutional setups. Consequently, those who had the desire for advanced education did not enter this category of schools. The fact that the road was closed for the vocational school graduates to go on for advanced education created a bias among the people towards the vocational education.

In this way the students completing the six-year primary education course can be divided into two large categories: (1) those who advanced to the secondary (middle) schools and (2) those who proceeded to the upper elementary schools and the youth schools. The diagram in p. 90 indicates the position and character of the various schools in secondary education before 1947.

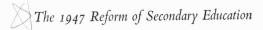 The 1947 Reform of Secondary Education

The report of the proposals made by the American educational envoys in 1946 concerning the reform of Japanese education dedicated a chapter for the reform of the secondary schools in Japan. Therein a suggestion was made that, as the existing system of secondary schools where students entered after six years of elementary school had been very complicated and had caused social distinctions among schools, the system should be changed in the following fashion: primary education should consist of six years, secondary education, three years, and a higher secondary school, also three years. This is known as the 6-3-3 system. The National Committee for the Reform of Japanese Education accepted this proposal which was materialized in three-year middle school and three-year high schools, forming a system of six years of secondary education. This took form in the inauguration of the 1947 School Education Law. This system made the previous double tracked system into a single track. This was a great change in the new system. Thereby middle schools became compulsory and along with elementary school they came to function as institutions of general education. The higher secondary schools to which middle school graduates enrolled came to be called high schools.

Thereafter, by the adoption of coeducation system the distinction of middle schools for boys and girls' high schools disappeared. The vocational education was given in the vocational course of the high schools or in vocational high schools. Thus, the division into three types of schools in the earlier secondary education system ceased to exist. Also the upper elementary schools and the youth schools which had been popular schools in the old system were integrated into the new system. The upper elementary schools converted to middle schools and the youth schools changed to part-time, evening schools and correspondence courses. Thus, the system and with it the distinction of schools, which had grown over a long period within the system of secondary education and the privileged connections which made possible advance to higher level schools, were swept away.

When the middle schools were organized under the new system, attendance immediately reached more than ninty-nine per cent, because from among the students who had already completed the six-year compulsory primary education course of the old system, the greater portion entered middle schools or the upper elementary schools, and those who did not attend some kind of secondary schools were extremely few. Again, as the new high schools were established by reforming the previous middle schools, all of them became the high schools of the new system. Consequently, the students then studying above the junior high schools became students in the lower grades of the new high schools. The transfer to the new school system progressed without confusion, and Japanese secondary education assumed a completely new dress.

Since 1962 a five-year special high schools have been newly institutionalized for the graduates of the new middle schools. This measure aimed at combining some high schools and junior colleges to provide an integrated education primarily for technological training. The following diagram illustrates the present school system:

At present almost all children attend the middle schools, as the middle school education became compulsory. There are about 12,800 middle schools with six million pupils and about 4,600 high schools. The number of high school students is increasing year by year. The number which had been about 1,620,000 in 1949 reached 3,230,000 in 1960, indicating a remarkable growth. This is owing to the fact that more middle school graduates tend to go on to high schools. Most recently more than

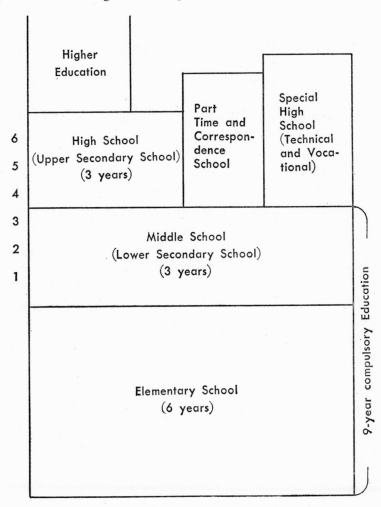

seventy per cent of middle school graduates advanced to high schools. The percentages of those going on from middle schools to high schools are given in the following list:

Year	Percentage
1950	45.5
1955	53.6
1960	60.2
1961	66.7
1962	65.2
1963	67.8
1964	70.6

The increases reflect a policy of attempting to have middle school graduates continue on to high schools. At this moment the increase has reached to such an extent that high school education may be called half-compulsory. However, since there are still those who have not yet had the opportunities of high school education among working young people, the government is considering various forms of education to meet their needs. The question of how to provide upper secondary education is being discussed. There are various problems such as the completion of high school through part-time or correspondence courses, the problem of high school education and vocational training within industries, and the problem of giving education to the youths in agricultural villages.

CHAPTER VIII

The Development of Higher Education

The modern Japanese school system was initiated by the expansion of elementary education. And as the number of its graduates increased, the middle schools were founded, and again because of the growing demands of the middle school graduates for higher education, the schools at this level were created. However, plans for higher education had already been made immediately after the Meiji Restoration along with the elementary and middle school plans. They were not designed after the lower schools were completed.

The school plans of the new Meiji government show that measures were taken for the establishment of higher educational institutions. As is mentioned above, such schools for higher education had previously been established by the nobles and warriors, and at the end of the shogunate, the influential lords in Japan were running schools for their retainers in their capital cities. The shogunate in Edo (Tokyo) also possessed a large scale institution for higher education. The new government of Meiji took over those various schools and reorganized them to fit its new principles. In March, 1868, the government decided that the Gakushûin which already existed in Kyoto at the end of the shogunate be reformed as a new college. Also in the new capital of Tokyo, the Shôheizaka Academy (for the study of Chinese classics), Kaiseijo (Western studies) and Igakukan (Western medicine) which had been administered by the Tokugawa shogunate were procured by the new regime and changed into colleges which functioned as the central organs for research and education. In February, 1870, the third year of the new regime, a university law was promulgated and a policy of founding a university with five departments was determined. The five departments were those of education, law, literature, natural science and medicine which were adopted from the European tradition of five arts. The students who entered this school were required to have had preparatory education at elementary and middle schools to enter the university, according to the law for those schools, which was promulgated simultaneously with the university law. Accordingly, Daigaku Honkô (University, Main Campus for Japanese and Chinese Studies), Daigaku Nankô (University, South Campus for Western Studies) and Daigaku Tôkô (University, East Campus for Medicine) were established where students were enrolled from different parts of the country on the basis of recommendation and their mastery of specialized subjects. According to the scheme of the government, two universities were to be established in Tokyo and Kyoto as the highest educational institutions in the eastern and western parts of the country respectively. To these were entrusted the entire educational policies of those districts. However, as the new government was transferred to Tokyo, plans for the university in Kyoto were temporarily abandoned, and the one in Tokyo was established first.

When the school system was founded in 1872, the three divisions of education at university, middle and elementary levels were set up. But in this system, no detailed provision was made for the organization of a university. It was stated only that the university was a school for special education of higher level in which four departments, natural science, literature, jurisprudence and medicine should be established. It was a system depending upon school districts. The university districts were designated in addition to elementary school districts and middle school districts. As eight university districts were planned, eight universities should have been established. It was, however, only in the year 1877 that the first daigaku, Tokyo University, was officially established as the highest organ of education in Japan. That means, for the five years after the Government Order of Education was promulgated, no university existed.

The school system of 1872 also made provision for colleges (*semmon gakkô* or technical schools) as organs of higher education. Only those who graduated from elementary school and studied foreign languages for two years at foreign language school were permitted to enter the college at the age of sixteen. After three years of preparatory course, students continued to study in their major field for two to four years more. In those colleges foreign teachers were to be hired to teach Western learning and techniques. They taught jurisprudence, medicine, astronomy, mathematics, physics, chemistry and technical science. There were colleges of veterinary medicine, commerce, mining engineering and mineralogy, different arts and sciences as well as technical colleges, medical schools and law schools. The Ministry of Education decided to start with those colleges for higher education and later to establish universities. As is mentioned above, the new system was applied to the existing colleges of early Meiji, and the new Tokyo Kaisei Gakkô and the Medical School (Igakkô) were made government schools. In 1875, 324 students were enrolled in the Tokyo Kaisei Gakkô and 488 in the Medical College. In addition, six colleges in the fields of agriculture, medicine and jurisprudence were created about that time.

In April, 1877, the Tokyo Kaisei Gakkô and the Medical College were amalgamated into Tokyo University which initiated the modern tradition of the Japanese *daigaku* or university. To the establishment of this school, an American advisor to the Ministry of Education, David Murray, made not a small contribution based upon his experience in American universities. Four departments of natural science, law, literature and medicine were established in Tokyo University, thus carrying out the provisions of the law of 1872. Students who wished to enter these departments were obliged to complete four years' general education in the preparatory school of the same institution. Each department of Tokyo University was again divided into sections for special studies. That is the department of science consisted of five sections, chemistry, mathematics-physics-astronomy, biology, technology and geology-mining engineering; the department of literature—the sections of history-philosophy-politics and Chinese-Japanese literature; the department of medicine—those of medicine and pharmacy; that of law—the section of jurisprudence. The period of study in those four departments was usually four years. Together with the four years of preparatory school, eight years were required at this university. In 1882 the university had 116 teachers and 1,862 students.

After 1877, the number of colleges gradually increased. In 1880 there were two government colleges, 32 public colleges and 40 private colleges. The total number of students enrolled in those schools was 5,072. After this time several private colleges for studies in law and economics were established in Tokyo where middle school graduates who wanted to continue their studies gathered and the number of students increased year after year. Some of those private schools were Tokyo Hô Gakkô (Tokyo Law School), Senshû Gakkô (School for Special Studies), Meiji Hôritsu Gakkô (Meiji Law School), Tokyo Semmon Gakkô (Tokyo Special College), Igirisu Hôritsu Gakkô (English Law School) and Doitsu Kyôkai Gakkô (German Society School). In 1885, 1,575 students were studying in six private law schools. Those law schools and commercial colleges were reorganized later into private universities. Most of the important private universities in Tokyo were established about that time as colleges.

In 1886, a large-scale reorganization of the school system was begun and special legislation was promulgated for Imperial universities. Also a law for normal schools was promulgated and provision for higher normal school education was established. The preparatory school was shifted from the university to the higher middle school and integrated into the middle school system. But in reality, they should have been considered a part of higher education. Later, they became independent and were called higher schools (kôtô gakkô). The Imperial universities were established under a special law with the objective of providing the education in science and technology needed for the country. Owing to the fact that the Imperial universities belonged to the state, this objective was stipulated in the provision. At that time the whole educational policy was planned for the sake of the country. The Imperial university was set to be the highest training organ of important government officials. In fact, many capable government officials and businessmen were the graduates of the Imperial universities.

According to this University Law, one Imperial university should be established in Tokyo which had several colleges (Bunka Daigaku) and graduate schools. In the former, academic or technical theories and application were to be taught. It was to consist of a law school, a medical school, a technical college, a college of liberal arts and a science school, to which were later added agricultural colleges, totalling six colleges. The president was assigned by the Minister of Education and administered the school. The minister also appointed two professors from each college as counsellors who formed the board where important matters related to school curriculum and other administrative affairs were discussed. The graduate school was for advanced studies, and the students after some years of study received doctor's degrees by examination. As to the advancement of degrees, the Law for Procuring Degrees was provided.

Under this system there was no possibility for the establishment of universities other than the Imperial Universities. Under the policy of the Ministry of Education, a gradual increase in the number of Imperial Universities was planned. In 1897 the second Imperial University was created in Kyoto and the original programme of the early Meiji period was embodied in the two universities, one in Tokyo and the other in Kyoto. Afterwards in 1907 Tôhoku Imperial University was established in Sendai; in 1910 Kyûshû Imperial University in Fukuoka and in 1918 Hokkaidô University in Sapporo, making a total of five Imperial Universities throughout Japan. Each of them consisted of several colleges. They made a considerable contribution both as institutions of higher education and as sites for progress in academic research.

Those who wanted to study in the universities were to undergo two years of courses in the senior division of the middle schools. These courses were in general education, preparatory for universities and were regarded as a part of the higher educational organ. This system was introduced by the educational reform in 1886 when seven higher middle schools were established in various parts of the country. According to that regulation, there were two groups of students: those who continued to study later in universities and those who, after graduation, went into practical work. For the former, general education was given; for the latter, such sections as law, medicine, engineering, literature, science, agriculture and commerce were provided.

After that in 1894 the Higher School Law was promulgated for specialized education at the higher level. The higher schools were those which were reorganized from the existing senior divisions of the middle schools. The middle school graduates entered those higher schools. The course of special studies was four years and the preparatory course for university was three years. In accordance with this reform, the sections of law, medicine and technology were set up in the higher schools. Thereafter, those governmental higher schools assumed the task of higher academic education in the local cities, equivalent to that of the Imperial University in Tokyo.

But the courses of special studies were not able to be developed under the higher school system and were abolished later. Only the preparatory courses for university survived. In 1900 the higher schools were again reorganized into three sections of general education which were preparatory for entering universities. Those who wished to study law and liberal arts were enrolled in the first section; the candidates for engineering, natural science and agriculture, in the second section; and those for medical schools, in the third section. Thus, the objective of the higher school as preparatory for Imperial Universities was attained, and institutionally universities were coordinated with the three-year higher school courses. That is, a six- or seven-year higher education system came into existence. It consisted of three years of general education at the higher school and three or four years of special studies in the university. In 1900, seven higher schools were established with 345 students. All of the graduates were later enrolled in Imperial Universities.

This system of higher education was considered the main course of higher education. The others were called *semmon gakkô* or special schools or colleges. Later, when the middle school graduates increased in number, only a selected portion of them were enrolled in the higher schools. As a result, the others who desired to go into advanced studies were obliged to take the courses of those special colleges. Many colleges of this category were established after 1900 and gave courses in various special subjects. Besides several important private colleges for the study of law and economics, the schools for languages, literature, art, music, national learning and religions were established. They were both governmental and private. In 1903, in order to coordinate many different colleges, a law for special colleges was promulgated. The establishment and management of those schools were subject to the control of this law, which stipulated that the special colleges were to teach advanced knowledge and techniques for more than three years to those who graduated from middle school. The terms and curricula of state schools were determined by the Education Minister. The regulations of each public and private schools other than the state schools were to be authorized by the same minister. Special attention should be paid to the fact that besides, those various colleges, women's colleges were established about that time for higher education in liberal arts and domestic sciences. In the meantime, although officially the Imperial University was the only university authorized by the education system of the time, several private colleges began to assume the name of university. Such schools as Tokyo Hôgakuin Daigaku, Meiji Daigaku, Hôsei Daigaku, Keiôgijuku Daigaku, Nippon Daigaku, Waseda Daigaku and so on had already the appellation of *daigaku* or university in this period. But institutionally they were treated as special colleges. Among other authorized colleges were such Buddhist schools as Tendai Shû Daigaku, Shinshû Daigaku, Bukkyô Daigaku, Sôdôshû Daigakurin and Nichirenshû Daigakurin. In other words, among these privately established higher educational institutions were special colleges, on the one hand, and on the other, those which were furnished with departments for higher academic or technical knowledge, assuming the title of *daigaku*. There were about fifty special colleges in 1905, of which 35 were private schools. The total number of students in that year was 25,054, of which 19,186 belonged to those private schools. Most of them majored in law, commerce and economics. Some studied medicine and religion. Those colleges where agriculture, engineering and commerce were taught were categorized as vocational colleges, distinguished from other special colleges. In 1905 there were 13 schools of this kind with 4,441 students, of whom 3,872 were enrolled in the vocational colleges of the state. Only 236 students attended private colleges in that year. This shows that special emphasis was laid on those vocational colleges by the government in order to promote vocational education.

A normal school was established in 1872 in Tokyo. After that, several governmental normal schools were created in principal cities of Japan in order to train elementary school teachers. These normal schools were established and administered by the state. In the year 1877, the local normal schools of the state were turned over to the management of the prefectural governments. But as the whole scheme of education was not very firmly organized, legally normal schools were not clearly defined. On the occasion of the educational reform in 1886, the ordinary normal schools and normal schools for the training of elementary school teachers and the higher normal schools for middle school instructors were institutionalized. At the normal schools, four years' education was given to those who graduated from upper elementary school or above between the ages of 17 and 20. In the higher governmental normal schools, the graduates of ordinary normal schools were enrolled for three years. Later, these ordinary normal schools were called simply normal schools and became prefectural and like other public middle schools, they were treated as equivalent to the middle school. In 1890 there were 47 normal schools with the enrolment of 5,295 students. In 1905 there were 66 schools with 18,924 students. Two higher normal schools were established in Tokyo; one for boys, the other for girls. In 1900 there were two of them with 803 students. The higher normal schools were organized as an integral part of the higher education programme.

As has been made clear, the establishment of these various schools was planned and carried out mainly from the time of the promulgation of the Government Order of Education in 1872 to the beginning of this century. The highest schools were the Imperial Universities. Other higher schools served as preparatory institutions for universities. Apart from those, special colleges and vocational colleges were created. The other lines of development was the schools for the training of teachers, such as normal schools and higher normal schools.

After World War I, as middle school education was substantially enlarged, it was also necessary to increase the higher educational facilities for the graduates. The basic principle was drafted by the Ministry of Education on the basis of the recommendation of the Extraordinary Education Council which was set up in 1917. Its purpose was the further development and reform of the higher educational system. The new scheme for higher school, university and college was initiated at this time.

The greatest reform was made in the system of higher schools. First of all, its preparatory function for entering the university was altered and the school was reorganized as an organ of higher, general education. The new higher school had two objectives: the education of middle class workers who might play a leading role in the development of the country in various professions after graduation and preparation for entering the university. Thereafter, the role of the higher school as an auxiliary to the university ceased to exist and the school became independent with an object of its own. It had four years of ordinary courses at the middle school level and three years of advanced courses, totalling seven years. From this we can see that the content of this higher school was an amalgamation of middle school courses and advanced courses. And at the same time, higher schools having only advanced courses were also established. The middle school had a five-year programme. But it was possible that after four years the students could enter this new higher school. Consequently, the first four years of the ordinary courses of the higher school were the course equivalent to those of the first four years of the middle school. In this manner, the years of schooling before entering the university were shortened. This higher school was composed of two sections, science and humanities. The selection of the two sections were optional. Thus, the higher school became an organ for the accomplishment of higher general education. Many higher schools were established successively and thereafter not all of the graduates advanced to the courses of the university. Accordingly, the number of higher schools and the students considerably increased. They were governmental and prefectural as well as private in nature. In 1918 there were only eight higher schools with 6,731 students; but in 1930, 20,551 students were studying in 32 schools.

As the higher school system was thus extended, the university system was also reorganized. In 1918 the University Order was issued for this purpose, in which the objectives of the university were defined as follows: "to teach theories and applications of learning and technique for the state and to make further research in respective fields and at the same time to develop personality and foster a patriotic spirit".

Eight departments of law, medicine, technology, literature, science, agriculture, economics and commerce were cited as organizational divisions of the university. Accordingly, the colleges which had been established in the Imperial Universities were abolished and the new departments or faculties were set up, so that each department might be able to function as an integral part of the university. In most cases, universities had several departments, but also those which had a single department were authorized to be called *daigaku*. Also research sections were to be created in each department. In order to facilitate the coordination of those sections, universities could have graduate schools. The terms of study in each department were to be more than three years with the exception of medical school (four years). The qualification for entering the university was ordinarily graduation from higher school, but depending upon the university, those who were considered as having equal or more ability were also accepted. Also the establishment of the preparatory courses was authorized. The term of study was three years for those who had finished the fourth year of middle school, and two years for the graduates of the same. Besides the state university, private, municipal and prefectural universities were also authorized by the Order. Women's universities were not recognized at that time, for it was thought that the time was not yet ripe. The highest educational organs for girls were special colleges.

After this reform in the university and college system was carried out, in addition to Imperial Universities, there were many colleges which, although they had assumed the name of *daigaku* or university, had not been treated as special colleges and were not authorized as regular universities. At the same time many municipal and prefectural universities were established in big cities. Thus, the total number of universities increased as well as the enrolment of students. In 1918 there were simply five Imperial Universities and 9,040 students, whereas in 1930 this increased to 46 universities and 69,605 students, enroled both in private and public schools. As a result of this increase in the numbers of universities and students, the primary purpose of establishing the Imperial University as an institution for an elite few had to be reconsidered.

In regard to special colleges, no special reform of the system was made but a programme for increasing the number of colleges and students was set up and carried out. Especially, owing to the fact that many girls who graduated from middle schools wanted to have higher education, women's colleges were created about this time, although they were not treated as universities. In the meantime, in order to meet the technological and industrial demands which came about as a result of World War I, the establishment of vocational colleges was planned. The creation of several schools of technology at the college level was one of the characteristic changes of the time. In 1918, in 96 vocational and technical colleges 49,348 students were studying, but in 1930 the number of schools increased to 162 with 90,043 students. Thus, those schools became the most influential among higher educational institutions, having the majority of schools and students.

As to normal schools, the number of middle school graduates who entered those schools gradually surpassed that of upper elementary school graduates. Accordingly, in 1931 the system was reorganized and a two-year course was established for the middle school graduates. This indicates that the normal schools for the training of elementary school teachers was approaching the level of college. Later in 1943, the duration of study in those normal schools was extended to three years and their status was changed to "college". Thereafter, all the training of teachers was to be carried out at the level of higher education. The development of the system for teachers' training in Japan was parallel to the extension of elementary education. The 52 normal schools with 15,639 students in 1900 increased to 105 schools with an enrolment of 43,852 students in 1930. There were two higher normal schools training teachers for middle and normal schools in 1900 with 803 students, but in 1930 there were four of them and the number of students went up to 2,773.

As is seen above, by the end of the 1930's the higher education system of Japan was determined in its scheme and scale. From about 1935 till 1945 those higher education organs were all expanded in number of schools and students. The statistics of various schools belonging to the category of higher educational organs in 1945 are as follows:

Higher schools   33 with 21,687 students;
Universities   48 with 98,825 students;
Colleges   172 with 121,901 students;
Vocational colleges   137 with 91,049 students;
Normal schools   56 with 56,261 students;
Higher normal schools   7 with 4,533 students;
Teachers' training institutes and normal school for youth
                        79 with 15,394 students.
In total there were 522 schools and 409,650 students.

After the Second World War an over-all educational reform was undertaken in 1947 and a 6-3-3-4 system was enacted with the result that most of the higher educational activities were to be carried out in the four years' courses of the universities. In other words, the various schools which had existed as higher schools, colleges, vocational colleges, normal schools, higher normal schools, other teachers' training institutes, etc. were amalgamated into a unitary system of higher education, the university. The universities which had existed before the war were also subject to reorganization under this new system. The general direction of the reform was to organize the various schools into one single category of university. Accordingly, various public colleges were changed into universities, each of which was established in its respective prefecture. Also in large private colleges and universities with preparatory courses, those colleges and courses were reorganized into departments or faculties, making comprehensive universities. This was the most important point of the reform.

Women's colleges were allowed to be called *daigaku* so that the door of entry to the university was open also for girls. At the same time those schools which had not had the setup necessary for being universities were integrated into the university system as junior colleges of two years.

Generally a four-year course was provided at the university for high school graduates, with the exception of the medical schools where the course of study required six years. Also a graduate school system was established for students desiring to pursue advanced studies. More than two years' study was required for the candidates for the master's degree and five years' study for obtaining the doctorate.

In 1957 ten years after the new system was inaugurated, the number of universities was 231; that of undergraduate students was 564,454; and that of graduate students 14,301. There were also 713,137 students registered in 269 junior colleges—all of this totalling 500 universities and colleges with 637,591 students.

In comparison to the pre-reform setup, the number of schools decreased, but the students attending them increased about 50%. Since then, both schools and students have increased considerably. At present the number of students enrolled in those schools has reached nearly one million. In recent years, owing to the demands of industry, higher technological schools of five years with three years' high school course and two years' advanced courses were also established. As a result, there are four types of schools in the field of higher education—universities with graduate schools, four-year universities; two-year junior colleges, and five-year higher technical colleges. It is expected that because of the postwar increase in population there may be a remarkable rise in applicants for universities after 1967. And the peak of the enrolment in those schools will be in the years 1967—1970. The government is considering measures for meeting this expected increase of students.

CHAPTER IX

The Advancement of Social Education

Social education in the modern period was begun after the establishment of the modern state of Japan in 1868. But the prototypes of such systems and activities can be traced far back to earlier times. The history of libraries, for example, shows that already in the Nara period Isonokami Yakatsugu had created Untei library. Also from earlier times young men's associations had been founded in rural areas. These were a type of guild for young people *(wakamono gumi)* which served as a kind of hostel and meeting place. In their constitutions *(okitegaki)* the rules of the principal activities of the individual groups were defined. It is said that the young people's groups were defined. It is said that the young people's organization of the post-Meiji period derived from these guilds of the Edo period. The organizations of young warriors of the Tokugawa period such as *gôchû* (country union) and *kumi* (group or guild) may be considered as the embryonic form of the modern boy scout movement. Another predecessor of modern social education is the *Shingakukai* or Society of Practical Ethics which functioned in the Edo period as a place of spiritual discipline for the social education of townsmen.

From these examples we may see that education for the general public, though not organized in the form of school, has long existed in Japan. However, these cannot be ranked with modern social education in the true sense of the word.

True social education as a positive programme was part of the framework of the modernized education system in that the social activities and services were, according to law, to be used for the purpose of the general cultural advancement of the nation. Among the earliest modern social establishments were libraries and museums. The first such public library was the one established at Yushima in Tokyo by the Ministry of Education in 1872. In the provision of the Order of Education of 1879, the establishment of libraries was listed along with that of the school system. It was stated that the libraries were to be under the direct control of the Ministry. In the same manner, several public libraries were opened in local districts. According to the annual report of the Ministry published in 1882, libraries, for example, the Osaka Prefectural Library, were established in twelve different prefectures. Several municipal and communal libraries, both private and public, were also founded. In 1899 the Library Act was promulgated, in which, for the first time, special regulation was made for the establishment of social education. Some time after that, more detailed rules for the establishment and administration of libraries were devised. Thus, we may see that the libraries were the earliest instrument of social education which appeared in the country.

In 1872, the first modern library was created in Japan, and in the same year, for the first time, an exhibition sponsored by the Ministry of Education was held. In 1877 a museum called the Education Museum was officially founded and opened to the public. In that year, outside of Tokyo, several other museums were inaugurated in such cities as Osaka, Kyoto, Kanazawa and Akita. However, though these were specific regulations for library administration, there were none for the administration of museums. They were simply to be supervised by the Ministry of Education as a part of the general programme of social education.

It was after 1910 that a general policy was arrived at for the advancement of the public education policy. The Ministry of Education took the initiative in giving guidance in various fields of social education. According to that programme, they were roughly divided into three categories of activities: (1) the compilation of and awarding of prizes to good reading materials, public libraries, itinerant libraries and exhibitions; (2) the selection and preparation of slides and movie films as well as the compilation of their accompanying explanatory texts; (3) lecture meetings and the compilation of lecture materials. A comprehensive system of modernized social education was thus begun by those political measures. Another area of this modernization effort was the fostering of youth organizations. For that purpose it was considered necessary to create a central organization which could coordinate the activities of youth groups all over Japan. The first national conference of young people was held in 1910 in Nagoya. About 1,500 representatives of different prefectures gathered together to discuss the development of youth organizations. There the rules and the outline of activities were drafted and a nation-wide policy for the establishment of youth organizations was made. After World War I, this youth organization was further strengthened. In 1915 the government sent instructions to each prefecture to encourage their establishment. Thereafter, many regional organizations were created in all the prefectures and a national federation was also established.

After World War I, the Extraordinary Education Congress was established to formulate basic principles of education. In 1918 the Congress brought to the attention of the government of the urgent need for the modernization of public education. This recommendation asked for the creation of administrative machinery for the development of public education and proposed to appoint specialists in the Ministry of Education and prefectural offices. Several proposals were made at the basic level of public education. These proposals included such things as good reading materials, the development of libraries and museums, the promotion of popular lectures, the improvement of the contents of movie films and other performing arts, the advancement of musical activities, the betterment of theatre and vaudeville installations, and the development of institutions for physical education. As the scope of public education covers various fields, it was proposed that central as well as regional administrative machinery should be established. In 1929 a Bureau of Social Education was established in the Ministry of Education. After that the facilities for various aspects of social education were substantially expanded. From that time on, the scope of activity of the Bureau was arranged and all of the activities and services of social education was categorized and gradually the different tasks of public education were made clear. They consisted of assistance to youth organizations, youth training centres, libraries, museums, and other exhibiting institutions, adult education, organizations for social betterment, authorization and recommendation of good publications and a few other areas. Through the expansion and development of these activities, new steps for the modernization of the education were taken.

During the years from 1920 to 1930, numerous instruments for public education were created and their activities gradually expanded. Among others, special emphasis was laid by the government upon the development of youth organizations and supplementary vocational training centres for young workers. These were the principal activities of public social education of that time. The youth organizations which were created in the prefectures consisted of many young agrarian workers. Those which were created on a community basis were related to prefectural centres, and were further controlled at the national level of the federation. Thus, this became the largest organ of social education in Japan. At the same time, for the young workers who could not attend school, supplementary training schools were established. There were about 15,000 such schools in the whole nation, and 1,270,000 workers attended them. Most of them attended the evening schools. In 1926 about 15,000 youth training centres were established by the Ministries of the Army and Education with the main objective of providing military training for young people. About 800,000 young men were enrolled in them. In 1935 the supplementary vocational training centres and the youth training centres were integrated into a new grouping called the school for young people (seinen gakkô). These were later expanded, and enrolment became obligatory for all the male population. It provided a five-year course for those who were not enrolled in middle schools and were engaged in practical work. Although they were called school (gakkô), they were considered organs of social education, established in existing educational institutions. After enrolment became obligatory, about 20,000 of them were established throughout the country. Some of them were created inside factories and other workshops and served as educational installations for the young people working there.

Similar establishments were created for the education of young women and formed an integral part of social education. Among them were the girls' organizations and the three-year youth school which, though not obligatory for girls, had an enrolment of 900,000 girls. They were run in a manner similar to the system exclusively for boys. In 1940 the national youth organization and the boy scouts' association were amalgamated into the National Youths' and Children's Organziation to serve the country under the war-time regime.

As to the education of adults, extension courses were given in various universities and colleges. They were called the Adult Education Lecture Series or the Citizen's University Courses. The lectures which were especially planned for women were called Family Lectures. Thus, existing school installations were gradually opened to the public for these programmes of public education. The adult education courses which were established in factories and workshops were called Workers' Courses. The models for them were the extension courses of foreign universities. But as the workers were obliged to attend schools outside of their places of employment, attendance was irregular and not much progress was seen in this field of activity.

Another organization similar to these adult education courses was the Mothers' Association. Cultural meetings for mothers of elementary school children were organized occasionally at girls' middle schools or elementary schools. For the most part, problems involved in children's education were discussed. Later, these groups were organized into mothers' classes and became more active.

Of all these instruments for social education, the earliest were libraries which gradually developed throughout Japan. The number of libraries which was over 1,000 in 1916 went up to 2,000 by 1921, and 4,300 by 1926. Here we may see that the number increased four times within ten years. At present there are approximately 4,700, of which 3,300 are public libraries. This indicates that most of them were established by prefectural and local communities.

During the same time, museums were inaugurated in different places as part of the programmes of modern social educational policy. But their number was limited and has not made progress comparable to that of the libraries. During these same years, recommendable books, films, slide pictures and records were designated by the Ministry of Education. During World War II, this kind of policy was pursued more strictly in order to control public thinking. The result was that those measures which had been introduced for the betterment of the cultural level of the nation were diverted into means of restricting freedom of public education and brought about negative effects.

After World War II, in an effort to improve the culture of the state following the principles of educational democracy, great emphasis was laid on the role of education outside the school. Under these circumstances, the conventional public education scheme was reexamined. Many proposals were made for the establishment of new organs and methodology. In order to make these changes, however, it was necessary to rearrange the legal provisions on public education in general. Along with the School Education Law, the Social Education Law was promulgated in 1949. Also, shortly after that, the regulations for libraries and museums was drafted. In 1950 the Library Law and in 1951 the Museum Law were enacted. Thus, several legal steps were taken for the reorganization of the scheme of public education.

One of the new creations within social education was the citizens' public halls (*kôminkan*). Those public halls were founded in municipalities and local communities for the use of the inhabitants of the districts. Each hall has furnished with assembly rooms, an auditorium and a library. About 3,000 of them were established in different parts of the country. Especially among the populations of farming villages and among fishermen and mountain people, they functioned as centres of public education. It is noteworthy that they have made a considerable contribution to the cultural, industrial and technical development of their respective areas in the post-war period.

One of the new activities of social education in the post-war period was the organization of youth classes (*seinen gakkyû*). They were the spontaneous gathering of young workers for studying some special subject. After finishing their study at middle schools, they were engaged in

various vocations, but in order to continue their study after their obligatory education of nine years, they organized these courses by themselves
in each area. They used citizens' public halls or the elementary or middle
school buildings and asked for lecturers to improve themselves. They
run these courses autonomously. These courses for young people were,
however, mainly established in agrarian and mountain villages. No
special law was made to cover these activities. In 1955 more than 17,000
courses were established throughout Japan, with no less than one million
young people attending them. The content of the courses was not only
general in nature, but also included subjects pertaining to the technical
development of local industry. For the purpose of assisting these classes,
the Ministry of Education drafted a Law for Promotion of Youth Classes
in 1953, under which they came under the responsibility of the educational programmes of municipalities and local communities and were
assisted financially from the public budget. Later, however, as the
emigration of the younger generation from rural areas into cities increased, the courses gradually decreased in number.

Another phase of the public education in the period after the war is the
active role of the Parents' and Teachers' Associations (PTA) which were
created in all of the schools in Japan. They were established in the elementary, middle and high schools and not only support schools, but also
serve as instruments of adult education. Ordinarily the parents of all the
children attending school participate in those associations, so that the
total number of associations is approximately 43,000 with a membership
of nearly 18,000,000. At present these combined associations form the
largest organizations of adult education in Japan. The Parents' and
Teachers' Associations deal with the problems of school affairs as well as
those concerning the guidance of school children. Through active discussion, they try to acquire new knowledge and methods. In some cases,
they hold lecture-meetings considering such subjects as problems of
education, culture and daily life. It should be noted that attendance at
these PTA meetings provides an opportunity for the cultural advancement of the parents, especially of mothers. Many courses were established
after the war for the education of women. It should be noticed that these

have served to liberate women from their conventional cultural isolation as female citizens. Besides the PTA, several other cultural courses have been organized for the benefit of women. Their appellations vary. Actually there are more than 30,000 courses for women with nearly 2,500,000 female in attendance.

Besides these, the larger, official institutions, organizations and activities were reformed after World War II and even expanded. Libraries and museums began to play a more active role, and gave wider opportunities for cultural development. Mobile libraries especially helped to increase the number of readers. In addition to books, libraries began to provide other materials of a cultural nature. They have, in fact, become local cultural centres.

Children's and young people's groups have also been reorganized. Especially noteworthy is the creation of youth homes and children's cultural centres. At the same time, there has been remarkable progress during the twenty years after the end of World War II in the expansion of correspondence courses and in the creation of audio-visual libraries, educational films and slides, and educational radio and television.

CHAPTER X

Education Policy and Its Problems

The national policy for education was institutionalized after the establishment of the modern state at the time of the Meiji Restoration. In actuality many schools had already existed before that period and some kind of education had been carried on in different institutions, but, owing to the lack of an integral policy covering the entire country of Japan, it had been impossible to plan a nation-wide education system. Therefore, there had been neither a unified form of education nor a setup for its central administration.

As soon as the new Meiji government was created, however, a plan was drafted for the creation of a new system of education for the entire country. First, a general principle was laid down for the establishment of schools devoted to the intellectual advancement of the nation, and the policy thereof was gradually made clear. Although the Ministry of Education had not yet been established, a general plan was made to divide the country into eastern and western school districts and to establish a university in each of them, one in Tokyo and the other in Kyoto, where all the schools of those two districts were to be respectively administered. Besides the doctors *(hakushi)* who were to be in charge of higher education and research, several administrative officials for the education of each district such as *bettô* (Imperial advisors), *taikan* (general superintendents), *daigaku daijô* (chancellors of universities) were appointed to carry out the education policy of the government.

In 1871 the provincial governments of the feudal *han* were abolished and the prefectures *(fu* and *ken)* were created, while the administration of the central government was also reformed. On that occasion the Ministry of Education was established as the central agency for carrying out the education policy of the government. After that it became the pivot of the education policy-making of the entire country. With the creation of this Ministry, it was decided in accordance with the principles of the new education policy that a new system of education for the whole nation was to be set up and that all schools were to be under the super-vision of the Ministry. In other words, it was made possible for all schools and organs of education, both public and private, to continue to exist under the administration of the Ministry, and conversely no education system might be able to exist thereafter which might not be affected by the system and policy established by the Ministry. Shortly after the Ministry of Education was founded, an investigation was made to formulate a new school system. The education schemes of different countries were studied   'ter this research, the Order of Education of 1872 was promulgatec in which the basic ideas of a school system for the modern state of Japan were made public for the first time. The first chapter of the Order includes a statement that all schools in Japan should be thereafter supervised by the Ministry of Education. This education policy based upon the centralized scheme of administration has not been changed even to the present day.

Seven years later, in the Education Law of 1879 it was made manifest that the Ministry of Education would not present any detailed provisions for the administration of local schools, but would give just the general principles, and that the practical application of those principles would be entrusted to the governors of the respective prefectures. There were cases, however, in which as a result of the liberalization of the adminis-tration policy for education some schools which had been newly created had to be abolished in certain regions. Consequently, in the course of time, more detailed provisions were made to strengthen the central supervisory function of the Ministry. In particular, the reform of the school system in 1886 gave more controlling power to the Ministry in all fields of education.

In 1890 the new system of cities, towns and villages was enacted and the education policy was to be carried out taking this new arrangement into account. Since then the policies of the Ministry of Education have come to be applied systematically through the network of regional administrative authorities.

In this manner the principle of a centralized administr   policy of education was always pushed forward so that all schools in japan came to be standardized and the content of education also became uniform. This centralization policy not only standardized the duration of courses and the scheme of schools of different grades and categories, but also the content of lessons had to be arranged in accordance with the principles established by the Ministry of Education.

In the early years of Meiji when the modern schools were founded, there was no formal education system and the subjects of lessons had not been determined. The materials and methods of teaching differed in each school. After about 1880 the curricula and the nature of subjects to be taught were determined by the Rules for Teaching. Each school was requested to give lessons in conformity with the rules. At the same time, the adoption of textbooks was to be authorized in each prefecture and unapproved texts were not permitted to be used. Later, it was required to obtain authorization for the use of textbooks in each subject. Thus, with developments in education the supervision of teaching material came under the control of the central government. In 1887 the system of the authorization of elementary school textbooks by the Ministry of Education came into existence. Thereafter, schools were obliged to use only those books which were authorized. Accordingly, the commercial publishers tended to compile textbooks based on the subjects and principles approved by the Ministry of Education and to apply for the authorization so that the content of textbooks gradually became standardized and the material similar.

Again, from about 1900, the Ministry of Education started a reexamination of the school system and more detailed provisions were made. This marked an epoch in the development of the school system which had been projected during the early days of Meiji. For each category of school, a school law was provided and detailed regulations for the carrying out of these laws were made. After that, the schools which belonged to the same category were established and administered by the same principles. The tuitions were also defined in the provision. Moreover, after 1903 all elementary school textbooks were compiled by the Ministry of Education. Consequently, all the elementary schools started to use the same kind of books. And the policy of selecting and approving educational materials by the government was thus accomplished.

As to middle schools and girls' high schools, not only were their curricula determined, but detailed instructions for lessons were given in regard to each subject and the teachers were requested to execute the contents of the instructions. Their textbooks were also to be authorized. Consequently, as all textbooks were compiled by private publishers according to government instructions, their contents were obliged to be standardized.

In this way, as the result of the centralization policy not only were the system and administration of schools standardized, but also the curricula and textbooks were so constructed that they conformed to the government policy of that time. This became even more evident after 1932 under the wartime regime. For example, the textbooks for middle school, girls' high school, and normal school which had been prepared by the authorization of the government became state textbooks and a single kind of textbook came to be used in all schools in Japan. The use of state textbooks for elementary school also continued. The teachers were instructed to give lessons in accordance with the teacher's educational guide prepared and distributed by the Ministry of Education. This fact shows very clearly the strong control of education by the govenment.

One of the basic principles incorporated in the Fundamental Law of Education which was enacted after the end of World War II was the decentralization of the administration of education. The reform was executed accordingly. The purpose was to weaken the control of the Ministry of Education and to strengthen the autonomy of prefectural and regional communities in the administration of educational affairs. The result was the creation of the Boards of Education which were institutionalized in 1948. It was a policy which had been hitherto unknown in Japan, but one which became one of the important pillars of postwar education reform. Following democratic principles, members of the Prefectural and Community Boards of Education were to be elected by direct public vote of the inhabitants. The duties of the boards were to prepare and administer the local education programme. The directors of education were to be appointed by the members of the board from among specialists. A supervisor was assigned for actual orientation and advisory services. Thus, the direct and centralized control of the Ministry of Education ceased to exist and only general guidance and advice were to be given by the Ministry to the local Boards of Education.

Such a decentralization policy was executed not only at the administration level, but also in the actual education programme of each school. The Ministry of Education provides the national standard for the subjects and their contents by issuing the *Guide for Courses of Study*. The Board of Education of each prefecture refers to it and makes the programme of the courses in the prefecture. In preparing them, special conditions of the region are taken into consideration. Again, referring to the general programme given by the Board of Education, each school in the prefecture plans a curriculum appropriate to the particular circumstances of the school. In this manner, schools have come to arrange their own teaching subjects and materials. It was called the curriculum movement and helped the development of new educational practices in all the schools in Japan. The state textbooks were abolished after World War II, and the system of authorization was restored for the use of elementary and middle school textbooks. Thus, different kinds of textbooks are being compiled and published again by private publishers. Besides the textbooks, various teaching materials were sought for and used in parallel with the textbooks upon the initiative of each school with the result that the educational materials for the use of both teachers and students have come to be much richer in content.

The principle of the decentralization of educational policy, however, was gradually amended as a tendency to centralization again came into being after 1950; but the basic character of the new education policy remained unchanged. Now that the strict intervention and control of the prewar regime have been severely criticized and have ceased to exist, the future problem is how to establish a liaison of education policies of the central and local governments. Particularly since the war the opinions of specialists have been taken into consideration in order to establish a fundamental education policy for the central government. The Central Council of Education, an advisory organization for the Ministry of Education, takes up important issues related to policy-making for education and has submitted several recommendations to the government. As to the orientation of courses at schools, the Curriculum Council was set up in the Ministry of Education. This agency examines the division of teaching subjects and the contents of curricula and submits positive measures for the improvement of education. Besides these two, twenty other advisory organs have been established to formulate the basic principles of policies and administration of education. Various committees and seminars have been organized in the local agencies of administration to collect the opinions and advice of teachers as well as local inhabitants to obtain the practical means of improving the education programme.

As is stated above, the school system in Japan has been developed to the extent that most of the younger generation are given opportunities for education. The compulsory nine-year course of elementary and middle schools accommodate more than 99% of the youth at the ages prescribed by the school law. More than 70% of the middle school graduates continue their study in high schools, which, as yet, has not become compulsory by Law. However, the statistics show that the number in high school attendance has so increased that it has become similar to the percentage attending high school under a compulsory education system. The students study there up to the age of eighteen. The number of high school graduates who enter higher institutions has also increased year after year. The total number of students who are enrolled in government, public and private universities and colleges reaches nearly one million. It can be said that there are a sufficient number of schools now in Japan to meet the demand of the population. The remaining problems of today are that of the expansion of pre-elementary education (kindergarten) and the supplementary education of the 30% of the middle school graduates who have gone into practical work after finishing the nine-year compulsory course. The problem of how to accommodate the overflow of applicants to the university may be one of the problems facing the school system and its administration.

Thus, the system of school education has been developed fully in number of schools and administration agencies, in relation to present needs. The future task of education policy-making is how to improve the quality of education. A series of problems must be considered and solved: establishment and installation of school buildings and facilities; supply of textbooks and other materials of education—especially the development and adoption of audio-visual equipment such as radio, television, educational films, etc.; reduction of the number of students per class to forty to effectuate an improved classroom situation; promotion of the quality of education in underdeveloped areas; provision of better facilities for handicapped children's education; and measures against juvenile delinquency. In the solution of these problems the teachers and administration officials play important roles. Therefore, the training and allocation of teachers are being reexamined. At present, those who graduate from four-year university courses and have the necessary number of credits required for teachers are granted the teachers' licences. Consequently, the teachers who are newly recruited are all university graduates, so that in twenty to thirty years the quality of teachers and the content of education may be considerably improved. In this respect, the task of the university as a training school for teachers is being reconsidered as one of the fundamental steps for the ultimate betterment of school education, and some positive measures are being proposed.

Although school education has been developed thus to the maximum in its institutional arrangement, the systematic and effective build-up of education outside school is much to be discussed in the future. As, hitherto, the policy of the government was centred in school education planning, the field of social education has not been fully built up nor its function well programmed. The development of a policy in this domain of education is expected to show substantial progress and will be incorporated in the programme of the national education policy. Several aspects of the social education policy are to be arranged to meet the needs of the nation: establishment of positive measures to arrange for education in enterprises for the majority of workers; organization and orientation of women's study groups in each region for their cultural development; development of education by correspondence; expansion of university lectures for local citizens; and improvement of the contents of radio and television which have been conspicuously developed in the past few years so that more effective education programming may be broadcast, and so on. It is expected that by the joint means of a more fruitful school education and a more effective social education the future policy will be planned and executed to meet the responsibility assigned to the government by the nation.

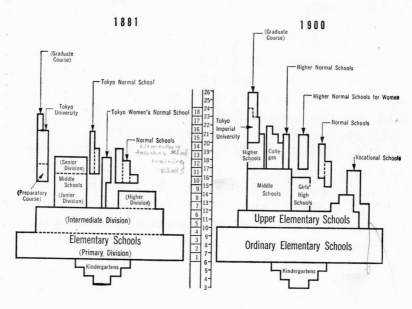
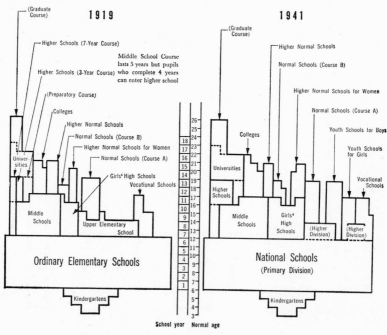

Chart I HISTORICAL REVIEW OF THE SCHOOL SYSTEM

Chart II   ORGANIZATION OF THE SCHOOL SYSTEM
1965

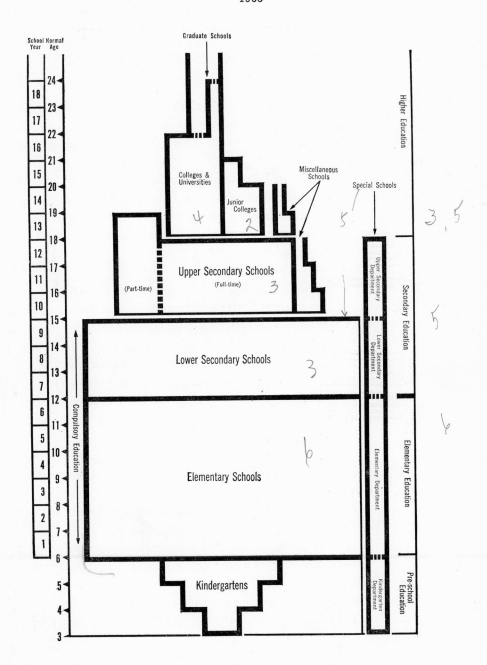

THE EIGHTY YEARS' DEVELOPMENT
OF JAPANESE EDUCATION

During the long feudal period under the Tokugawa regime, Terakoya—private schools, originally shrine (tera) schools, where the three R's were taught for the common people—and other educational establishments had developed.

"Government Order of Education" promulgated in 1872 established the first system of public education in Japan. This system was the foundation of modern education in this country. Since then, through frequent changes and developments, the modern democratic school system of today has been established.

The period of introducing the modern educational system. (1872–85)

 1872   The Government Order of Education was promulgated. By this Order the school system was organized in three progressive stages of elementary school, middle school and university. Thus, the modern educational system was introduced.

The period of systematizing the modern educational system. (1886–98)

 1886   The Elementary School Order, Middle School Order, Imperial University Order and Normal School Order were issued, and fundamental educational institutions—elementary schools, middle schools, normal schools and imperial universities—were organized. Three or four years of elementary education were made compulsory.

 1894   The Higher School Order was issued and higher schools were organized.

 1897   The Teacher Education Order was issued and normal schools and training colleges were organized as teacher training institutions.

The period of consolidating modern educational system. (1899–1916)

 1899   The Girls High School Order and Vocational School Order were issued and girls' high schools and vocational schools were organized.

1900   The period of compulsory attendance was extended to four years throughout the country and tuition in public elementary schools was abolished.

1903   The College Order was issued and colleges were organized.

1908   The course of the ordinary elementary school was extended from four years to six years and these six years were made compulsory.

The period of extending the educational system. (1917–39)

1918   The University Order and the Higher School Order were issued and universities and higher schools were reorganized. These Orders provided for the government's recognition of private and local universities and higher schools in addition to those established by the government itself.

1935   The Youth School Order was issued and part-time youth schools were opened as educational institutions of working youth.

1939   Youth school attendance was made compulsory for boys aged 12–19 years.

The period of wartime education. (1940–45)

1941   The National School Order was issued and elementary schools were renamed "National Schools". National schools were organized with six years of primary division and two years of higher division and an expansion of compulsory education to include the seventh and eighth grades was planned but not put into effect.

1943   The normal school system was reorganized. Since then, all elementary teacher training courses have been of college level.

The period of building up a new democratized educational system. (1946–   )

1946   The first report and recommendations of the U.S. Education Mission were submitted.

1947   The new Constitution was adopted, the Fundamental Law of Education, and the School Education Law were promulgated and the so-called 6-3-3-4 new system was established with nine years of elementary and lower secondary education being made compulsory.

1948   Special education for the blind and the deaf was made compulsory.

1949   The Private School Law was promulgated and education in private schools was promoted.

1950   The second report and recommendations of the U.S. Education Mission were submitted.

In Chart I are shown the educational structures in Japan at four periods prior to the postwar reorganization: in 1881, in 1900, in 1919, and in 1941.

Data from: Historical Review on Eighty Years' Development of Educational System, *Ministry of Education*